MAKING THE GRA

A Grading Guide to the Top 25 Most Widely C   U.S. Coins

By Beth Deisher

with coin grading
by
Michael Fahey
and
ANACS staff

Color Imaging: Lori Billing
Coin Photography: Garry Leapley
Designer: Cinda McAlexander

Acknowledgments:

Coins provided for photography by

ANACS: Morgan dollars.
Jack H. Beymer: Liberty Head 5 cents, Barber quarter dollars, Seated Liberty dimes.
Tom Bush: Barber half dollars.
Delaware Depository Services Co.: Saint-Gaudens double eagles.
Tony Cass: Standing Liberty quarter dollars.
Lee Crane, L&C Coins: Eisenhower dollars, Barber quarter dollars, Barber half dollars.
Michael Faraone: Walking Liberty half dollars, Standing Liberty quarter dollars, Indian Head cents, Winged Liberty Head dimes, large cents.
Michael Fuljenz, Universal Coin & Bullion: Coronet double eagles.
Harry Laibstain, HLRC: Barber half dollars.
John McCloskey: Seated Liberty dimes.
Tom Reynolds, Early American Coin Gallery Inc.: Large cents.
SilverTowne: Saint-Gaudens double eagles.
Andy Skrabalak, Angel Dee's Coins: Indian Head cents.
Richard Snow, Eagle Eye Rare Coins: Flying Eagle cents.
Jeff Starck: Roosevelt dimes.
Norm Talbert, The Great Lakes Company: Indian Head 5 cents.

Contents

Published by Amos Hobby Publishing, P.O. Box 150, Sidney, Ohio 45365-0150.

Publishers of *Coin World, Coin World's Coin Values, Coin World's Paper Money Values, Linn's Stamp News, Cars and Parts Magazine, Corvette Enthusiast, Mustang Enthusiast, Musclecar Enthusiast, Pontiac Enthusiast, Scott Stamp Monthly,* and the Scott Publishing line of philatelic catalogs and albums.

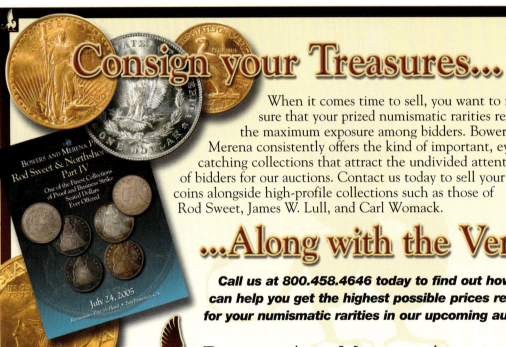

Grading Matters

The grade of a coin matters.

It matters because a coin's grade, or level of preservation, is a major factor in determining its value. (The other major factor in valuing a coin is rarity.)

In today's U.S. coin market, a basic understanding of grading is essential. What one pays for the collectible coin he or she purchases or expects to be paid for the collectible coin when selling will ultimately hinge on the coin's grade. In fact, many collectors and dealers will tell you that grade is just "shorthand" or a tool for communicating value.

Currently, U.S. coins are graded on a scale of 1 to 70. In grading, 1 represents the worst state of existence and 70 represents perfection, the absolute best state of existence.

The first 59 numbers are reserved for coins that have been circulated – those that have received wear as a result of having been passed from hand to hand or that have jingled their way through coin-operated machines. Consequently their state of being – preservation – varies widely. Numbers and adjectives are used to identify commonly accepted benchmarks describing their state of preservation and to convey information used in determining value.

Eleven numbers – 60 through 70 – are used to describe coins that have not been circulated. Some collectors refer to them as Uncirculated. In grading terms, they are known as Mint State. That is, the coins are just as they were struck by the press at the Mint, the government facility in which they were manufactured. If a coin has not been circulated, it cannot exhibit evidence of wear. However, a Mint State coin can have imperfections and it can be weakly struck and lack details.

The mastery of grading, especially the Mint State range, requires an understanding of and knowledge about what the perfect coin would be in each design and denomination and being able to discern the 10 increments that separate perfection (70) from the lowest grade of Mint State (60).

Grading mastery entails years of practical application (viewing many coins) and committing vast amounts of knowledge about coins to memory. That's why grading is commonly called an art. It is heavily dependent upon one's ability to view, remember and then judge each new coin by the memory of what has been seen before.

For centuries, the buyer and seller in direct negotiation determined the value of a coin. Most often, transactions were conducted face-to-face. With the advent of auctions and conducting transactions by mail, the need arose for a standard way of describing the coin and arriving at an agreed upon price.

The popularity of coin collecting and the explosion of mail-order transactions that began in the 1950s and accelerated dramatically in the early 1960s led to the publication of several books about grading. By the mid-1970s attempts to arbitrate between buyer and seller through the means of a grading opinion rendered by an unbiased, third-party gave rise to a new business known as a grading service, which for a fee would both authenticate and render a grade opinion on coins.

1986 witnessed the introduction of the "slab," a sonically sealed, tamper-resistant plastic holder designed to keep the grading opinion with the coin as well as to display and protect the coin. 1986 also marked the first full use of the 1 to 70 scale, with the first practical use of the 11 grades within the Mint State range and professional graders willing to back their grading opinions with a money-back guarantee.

Today coin grading is a highly competitive business. Unregulated, third-party grading services staffed by expert professional graders assign grades to millions of U.S. coins yearly.

Overall, third-party grading has brought a measure of standardization to the marketplace and is unquestionably an impetus for the current unparalleled growth in coin buying and selling in the United States, especially for coins valued above $100.

The existence of third-party professional grading services, however, doesn't preclude the need for individual collectors to understand the basics of coin grading.

While this book cannot make you an expert coin grader, it can begin to help you understand what is involved in grading a coin.

One of the most understandable explanations of what is involved in grading coins is contained in James L. Halperin's book, *How to Grade U.S. Coins*, which he has made available free of charge on the Internet at **www.coingrading.com**. (The printed version is available for sale at **www. Amazon.com**.)

Although Halperin's primary focus in the book is grading Uncirculated and Proof coins, his approach provides a foundation to understanding the key elements of grading, regardless of grade. He identifies four key components.

They are surface preservation, strike, luster and eye appeal.

Surface preservation refers to the condition of the surfaces (obverse or "heads side" and reverse "tails side") of the coin. For Uncirculated coins, close inspection will reveal contact marks from where the coin has collided with other coins or objects. Sometimes you find tiny scratches referred to as "hairlines" created by abrasive substances or material used in cleaning. Some coins are simply abused or mishandled. Imperfections could also be evident that were created on the coin's surface during various stages of its manufacture.

In analyzing the state of the surfaces of an Uncirculated coin one must weigh the visual impact of these imperfections and weigh the degree of severity and whether the locations of the imperfections seriously detract from the coin's overall appearance. A rule of thumb to keep in mind is that the smaller the diameter of the coin, the more detrimental scratches and nicks are on the surface of the coin. Larger diameter coins have a greater propensity for receiving scratches, nicks and marks. Unless such marks land in the prime focal areas of the designs, they do not affect the grade as much as if on a smaller canvas.

For circulated coins, the focus is on wear, or how much of the surface and design of the coin remain. To understand what is missing, one must be fully knowledgeable about what the coin would look like when newly struck and Uncirculated.

If wear can be detected on the surface of the coin, it is automatically classified as circulated. The best way to determine wear is to identify the design high points and inspect them for evidence of disruption in the surface. Tilt the coin from side to side and then slightly on the up-and-down axis. Silver coins with the slightest wear will evidence "gray areas" at the high points of the design. On copper and gold coins, the surface appears darker. The change in color and texture of the surface is an indication of a definite loss of luster, which is the first sign of wear. In grading parlance, it is referred to as "signs of abrasion on the high points," and often relegates coins that are mark-free and eye appealing enough to warrant a Mint State 63 grade back to About Uncirculated 58.

On the Uncirculated coin, the full luster will roll over the high points. On the AU coin the luster will be visibly broken and can be seen without magnification. Even the inexperienced eye will be able to discern slight wear, which is actually the displacement of metal.

One critical point to remember: Many Mint State coins may have slight "friction" on the high points or in the fields. It is the result of coins rubbing against each other in rolls or bags as they were packaged for distribution at the U.S. Mint. If the metal is not disturbed and the luster is intact, the coin is probably still Mint State.

Various benchmarks on the circulated grading scale from 1 to 59 denote how much of the original design remains. Often the description associated with a specific grade level will point to specific design devices as a point of reference. For example, many of the U.S. coin designs that feature a female personification of Liberty depict her wearing a headband or tiara with the word LIBERTY inscribed on it. One grade may be pegged at being able to read three letters of LIBERTY. The next higher grade level may cite five letters as the critical benchmark. The next higher level may require that the entire word be readable. Then,

the next higher grade may require that the word be not only be readable but bold.

While many consider grading circulated coins easier than grading Uncirculated coins, both require that the grader have an intimate knowledge of the coin's design elements.

Strike refers to the sharpness and completeness of detail imparted by the die when the planchet (blank disk) becomes a coin. A fully struck coin exhibits all of the elements of the coin design to the smallest detail. It is essential for anyone attempting to grade a coin to know what is supposed to be present on the coin – the design as fully struck. At various times, all of the United States minting facilities had striking problems. So, it is important to identify the striking characteristics of each Minting facility for each series.

Coin enthusiasts and researchers over the past 40 years have published books on nearly every series, detailing the characteristics and the idiosyncrasies of each date and Mint mark in a given series. Such research is especially helpful in alerting graders to weak strikes.

Weakness in strike does not by itself lower a coin's grade. But often, beginning collectors confuse weak strikes with slight wear. If the luster is

intact, odds are you are looking at a weak strike rather than a coin that has experienced wear.

Luster is created on a coin's surface from the microscopic flow lines as the metal flows to fill the die in the striking process. Once the coin is struck, the brilliance of the luster is created by the way the metal reflects light. The natural sheen, often referred to as "cartwheel" luster on larger silver coins, is highly desirable, to the point of the unscrupulous attempting to recreate it mechanically on coins that have lost their luster due to wear or cleaning.

Eye appeal is simply the aesthetic appeal of the coin, which is the most subjective factor. Overall attractiveness forces the grader to take all of the coin's qualities into consideration and rank and balance them.

In grading the Mint State coins, Halperin ranks surface preservation as the single most important factor, assigning it a weight of 40 percent. He weights the other three factors – strike, luster and eye appeal – at 20 percent each, or each half as important as surface preservation.

How to use this book

The information and photos published herein

constitute a learning guide, not a grading standard. They have been adapted from (and in some cases expanded upon) "Making the Grade," a regular column published in *Coin World's Coin Values*, a monthly magazine published by Amos Hobby Publishing.

In each issue of *Coin Values*, "Making the Grade" focuses on a specific series of U.S. coins, exploring the basics of grading – presenting tips, word descriptions for specific grades and color photos of specific grades. The column has focused on the most popularly collected series of U.S. coins.

Our intent has not been to necessarily present all grades possible of every series. Rather, our focus has been practical, featuring the most widely collected grades in each series.

Our approach is solidly visual because of our belief that seeing the coins in the various grades is one of the best ways to understand grading. The edge that a dealer or advanced collector has over a beginning collector is the number of coins he or she has had the opportunity to see. A big part of learning to grade is educating one's eyes (and mind) as to what should be present or not present for a specific grade. The next best substitute for

having the ability to inspect thousands of coins is to see sharp, crisp color images of coins that are representative of the various grades for any particular series of coins.

To ensure that the photographs are true to the grades, we obtain coins that are "solid for the grade" examples.

On occasion we have purchased the coins in the marketplace. But most of the coins have been loaned for photography by dealers or collectors who specialize in the series.

All coins selected for photography are personally graded by Michael Fahey, senior grader and authenticator for ANACS, or another member of the ANACS staff.

ANACS is a third-party commercial grading service located in Dublin, Ohio. At the time *Coin Values* was launched, both the magazine and ANACS were owned by the same parent company, Amos Press Inc. ANACS was sold to Anderson Press Inc. in April 2005, but Fahey and the ANACS staff have continued to confirm grades and assist in formulating grade descriptions on a consulting basis.

All coins are photographed in *Coin World's* studio in order maintain quality and consistency

in presentation. While it is not possible to show all of the characteristics one may see if the coin were held in one's hand and tilted or rotated under a light, the photograph captures most of the elements necessary in grading.

Each series is introduced with a short grading primer, followed by "color maps" and obverse and reverse illustrations that show the design high points.

The "color maps" depict Visual Impairment Severity Levels created by James L. Halperin. They are published in the magazine column and in this book through a special licensing agreement.

Location and severity of imperfections are key to determining the status of a coin's surface. Halperin, through the creation of color-coded "coin maps," helps you understand just how much they matter.

In each of the illustrated color-coded maps RED is considered Worst (Average x 4), ORANGE is Bad (Average x 2), YELLOW is Average, GREEN is Better (Average x 1/2) and BLUE is Best (Average x 1/4).

Halperin points out that his quantifications are approximate and explains that a mark in the red area is about eight times more serious than if the same mark were in the green area. The worst place for a mark or scratch is the focal point of the coin, colored in red. He also notes that the direction of the mark can increase or decrease its effect. For example, a vertical contact mark might be more obvious on certain design devices than a horizontal mark. A horizontal mark would be less noticeable because it would be somewhat hidden and at first glance may appear to be part of the design.

According to Halperin: "The least detrimental area to have an imperfection is on the rim. Rim imperfections tend to be less detracting and less noticeable, because the rim is the least important part of the coin's total design."

The design high points are highlighted in red and help you pinpoint where to look first for evidence of wear.

In some cases, close-up photos of some design elements are shown, especially if they are critical factors in grade determination.

Color photographs of both the obverse and reverse of each coin in the specific grade level are accompanied by the grade designation and a brief description of significant grade determinants.

Regardless of which series you choose to grade, we recommend that you spend time looking at and studying the photos of the highest grades presented for the series. Becoming familiar with the design and its intricate details should be your first step. Remember, every coin is a work of art. Its design was sculptured and it has three dimensions, even if it was struck in low relief.

Grading, although seemingly scientific, is subjective. There is an art to grading. Those who spend time honing their grading skills through observation and study are the most successful. It is a valuable and necessary skill for full enjoyment of collecting and/or buying coins in today's world.

An additional tip

Once you move from looking at the pictures in this book to picking up coins to grade, be sure you know how to properly hold your coin. The last thing you want to do is change your coin's state of preservation by improperly holding it.

By using the proper method, you can be sure you won't leave any trace of fingerprints, skin acids or oils or other damage while examining your coins or those of other collectors.

Damaged coins tend to have reduced eye appeal, thus receiving lower grades and reduced monetary value.

Why all the fuss about how to hold a coin? The acid or other naturally occurring chemicals on your fingertips can leave a residue on a coin's surface that doesn't go away and can't be removed without damaging the coin. Fingerprints

The proper way to hold coins is by the edges between the thumb and forefinger wearing a pair of light, cotton gloves. The gloves will protect the surface of the coin from oils and other contaminants on one's fingers that can be transferred onto the edge.

you see on some coins are the result of improper handling.

Improper handling can do more than leave naturally occurring chemicals on a coin. It can cause abrasions, decreasing the value of the coin itself and exposing fresh metal that can oxidize and corrode.

You also need to be careful where you lay a coin down. Be aware of the surface. Is it clean? If not, the coin may pick up contaminants.

So what is the best way to examine a coin? The answer is carefully and only when necessary.

The best way to handle a coin is while wearing clean, white cotton gloves. They are available in most coin supply stores. Touching the surfaces ungloved may result in fingerprints being left on your coins.

Once you've put on your gloves, the proper way to hold a coin is with the edge held securely between your thumb and forefinger.

If you don't have the gloves, it is even more important to hold your coin by the edge to minimize your physical contact with the coin. If you must touch a coin barehanded, be sure to wash your hands thoroughly with hot, soapy water before you begin.

Before you don the gloves and pick up the coin, put down a layer of newspapers and top the newspapers with felt to prevent accidental dings, bumps and scratches. Such precautions will eliminate or minimize damage, if you happen to drop the coin.

Don't lift the coin any higher than necessary to make your examination. The higher you the hold the coin, the bigger the bounce if it's dropped.

Some professionals go so far as to recommend wearing a cloth, surgical or paper dust mask when examining coins close up. The mask acts as a barrier between the moisture in your breath and the coin's surface. Moisture can cause spots on the metal.

Plastic encapsulations – whether from a third-party grading service or a coin supplies vendor – can offer protection against improper or frequent handling.

Remember you are custodian of your coins for a little while. Some day another generation of collectors will want the opportunity to own your specimen. So preserving your coins to the best of your ability is in everyone's best interest. Proper handling while grading or viewing your coins pays big dividends.

KEY TERMS

GRADING ABBREVIATIONS
AG About Good
G   Good
VG Very Good
F   Fine
VF   Very Fine
EF   Extremely Fine
AU About Uncirculated
UNC   Uncirculated
MS Mint State
PF   Proof

ABBREVIATION KEY
B   Brown
RB Red and Brown
R   Red
C   Cameo
D   Deep Mirror Prooflike
DC Deep Cameo
B   Full Split Bands (Winged Liberty Head "Mercury" dime)
F   Full Bell Lines (Franklin half dollar)
H   Full Head (Standing Liberty quarter)
FS   Full Steps (Jefferson 5 cent)

Large Cent

Large cents were the United States' first coins minted in quantity for general circulation at the nation's first Mint in Philadelphia. Produced from 1793 through 1857, these 100 percent copper coins with a diameter of 28.5 millimeters are just slightly larger than our present-day small dollar coins.

Collectors generally separate large cents into three distinct classifications: Early Dates (1793 to 1814), Middle Dates (1816 to 1839) and Late Dates (1840 to 1857).

The Early Dates and Middle Dates are passionately collected, but because fewer have survived they tend to be more expensive than the Late Dates, which are widely collected primarily because they are readily available and less costly. Thus, our discussion of grading large cents focuses on the Late Date coins, referred to by many as the Modified Coronet or Braided Hair cents. We use the grading system and terminology employed by the commercial third-party grading services, which adhere to "market grading."

Collectors and dealers who specialize in early copper coins often use a grading system devised by the Early American Coppers club known as "EAC grading." While EAC grading uses the same nomenclature, the grading is stricter and more technical in nature than market grading. Recent comparative studies have shown that in general EAC and commercial graders tend to agree on the lower grades from Poor 1 to Fine 12, but differ dramatically in the Fine 12 through About Uncirculated 58 grades. EAC grades tend to run about two points lower than commercial grading in the Mint State range. The point at which the two grading systems appear to agree is price.

The obverse design on the large cents of 1840 through 1857 is the work of Mint Engraver Christian Gobrecht, who adapted Robert Scot's head of Liberty, introduced in 1816, wearing a coronet or small crown with the word LIBERTY boldly engraved on it.

Gobrecht's left-facing portrait depicts a younger female with a slightly different hairstyle than appears on the Middle Date cents. While Scot's Liberty features long curly hair cascading from the coronet, Gobrecht's Liberty sports a fashionable braid across her forehead in front of the coronet. Scot's Liberty wears her long hair in a loose roll on the back of her head, held in place by a plain cord. Gobrecht's Liberty wears her hair in a tighter bun, held in place by a beaded cord, with dangling back curls that cascade around and under the truncated neck.

Gobrecht also modified the Wreath reverse design created by John Reich in 1816. Gobrecht's reverse modifications are more subtle than his obverse changes. His reverse changes include slightly enlarging the wreath and making the lettering of the ONE CENT and UNITED STATES OF AMERICA legends bolder.

When Late Date large cents were first struck they emerged from the dies with a brilliant red-orange surface. This is the color collectors call "red" and is abbreviated as RD or R. Exposure to the atmosphere induces oxidization, which produces change in color. This mid-range is known as "red and brown" and abbreviated RB. Often specialists denote percentages of red remaining, such as 90 percent, 50 percent, 30 percent and 10 percent.

Over time, especially if exposed to actively circulating air or placed into contact with materials containing sulfur (most paper and cardboard albums), the surfaces of large cents gradually turn brown. When no trace of red is detectable, the color is described as brown, abbreviated BN or B.

Color is an essential factor in grading copper coins and it must be taken into account to a much greater extent than with other metals. Also, spotting is taken into account as part of the "surface preservation grade" as well as the "eye appeal grade." A good rule of thumb to use for copper coins that are in all respects equal except for color would be to subtract two points from the surface preservation grade if the coin is brown and add two points if the coin is full red.

In the large cent map RED is considered Worst (Average x 4), ORANGE is Bad (Average x 2), YELLOW is Average, GREEN is Better (Average x 1/2) and BLUE is Best (Average x 1/4). A mark in the red area is about eight times more serious than if the same mark is in the green area. The worst places on the obverse for a mark or scratch are on Liberty's face and the date. On the reverse, the worst places for scratches and marks are on the center field containing the one cent denomination legend. (Copyright 2005, HeritageCoins.com)

Wear is detected first on the high points of the coin's design, which are highlighted in red. High points on the obverse of the Modified or "Braided Hair" Coronet large cent are the hair just in front of and above Liberty's ear, her eyebrow and her cheek. Design high points on the reverse are on the center parts of the leaves and the knot of the bow at the bottom of the wreath.

VG-8: Well worn over all. Coronet head of Liberty is clear but flat and lacks design details. Obverse: Details of Liberty's hair clear only in spots, mostly around bun at the back of head. LIBERTY on the coronet worn, but complete. The coronet is outlined, hair cord shows clearly. Wear evident on Liberty's cheek, neck. Reverse: Legends complete but some letters may be weak. Bold outlines of leaves, stems and bow on wreath show.

F-12: Moderate to heavy even wear. Obverse: Liberty's hair is worn from top of head to bottom of neck, some hair detail visible. Wear evident on Liberty's cheek. Wear detectable on upper edge of coronet. LIBERTY is bold. Beads on hair cord are sharp. Stars and date worn but sharp. Reverse: Leaves and bow on wreath heavily worn, but edges and some details show. Legends worn but bold.

VF-20: Moderate even wear evident on coin, especially on Liberty's cheek and neck. Obverse: Hair worn in spots from top of Liberty's head to upper neck, although most details are sharp. Remainder of hair and coronet are distinct. Curls on shoulder are flat. Reverse: Leaves of wreath are worn at high points, showing half of the details. Bow at bottom of wreath is well worn.

VF-30: Light even wear detectable on coin, but all major features are sharp. Obverse: Hair details above Liberty's ear are weak. Hair below the neck is worn, as are cheek and neck areas. Slight flatness detectable at tip of coronet. Reverse: Although some detail shows, leaves of the wreath are worn at high points. High points of bow are visible, but worn.

EF-40: Light wear evident on highest points of the obverse and reverse designs. Obverse: Wear visible at the top of Liberty's head, on her cheek, above her eye, to the right of her ear, at the tip of the coronet and along the high curls on her shoulder. Reverse: Slight wear evident on high parts of the bow and most of the leaves within the wreath.

EF-45: Very light wear on design high points. Obverse: Liberty's hair is very detailed. Wear shows above Liberty's ear and on parts of the hair above her eyebrow, on her cheek and her neck and below the end of her neck. Reverse: Slight wear shows on most of the leaves and on the bow.

AU-50: Trace of wear detectable on design high points. Obverse: Traces of wear on Liberty's cheek, near her ear, and on high points of curls on her neck and below end of her neck. Reverse: Slight wear on high points of leaves as well as the edges and ribs of the leaves. Trace of wear on the bow. Surface is somewhat lustrous.

AU-55: Small trace of wear shows on design high points. Obverse: Slight trace of wear on cheek. Trace of wear above and to the right of Liberty's ear. Reverse: Trace of wear present on high points of a few leaves within the wreath. Some Mint luster remains.

AU-58: Minute trace of wear on design high points. Obverse. Very slight signs of abrasion on hair above Liberty's ear. Reverse: Slight sign of abrasion on high points of leaves and bow of ribbon at bottom of wreath. Considerable Mint luster evident.

MS-60: Strictly Uncirculated coin with no trace of wear. May have large detracting contact marks and spots. Could have heavy concentration of hairline scratches or large areas of unattractive scuffmarks. May have rim nicks. Eye appeal is generally poor with unattractive or dull Mint luster. Color is dark brown.

MS-63B: Mint State coin with attractive Mint luster. May have noticeable detracting contact marks and minor blemishes. Small hairline scratches are visible without magnification. Coin has toned completely brown.

MS-63RB: Mint State coin with attractive Mint luster. May have noticeable detracting contact marks and minor blemishes. May have small hairline scratches. Surfaces exhibit combination of red and brown.

MS-64B: Mint State coin with average Mint luster. May have several small contact marks in groups as well as one or two moderately heavy marks. One or two small patches of hairlines may show under low magnification. Overall, coin is attractive with pleasing eye appeal. Color is completely brown.

MS-64RB: Mint State coin with average Mint luster. May have several small contact marks in groups as well as one or two moderately heavy marks. One or two small patches of hairlines may show under low magnification. Overall, coin is attractive with pleasing eye appeal. Some brown in color but exhibits good deal of red.

MS-65B: Mint State coin that exhibits full Mint luster and a sharp strike. A few barely noticeable nicks or marks may be present. Overall quality is above average and overall eye appeal is very pleasing. Color is completely brown.

MS-65RB: Mint State coin that exhibits full Mint luster and a sharp strike. A few barely noticeable nicks or marks may be present. Overall quality is above average and overall eye appeal is very pleasing. Color includes some brown but contains good deal of red.

Flying Eagle Cent

America's first small cent struck for circulation – the Flying Eagle cent – offered a new alloy but reprised designs from earlier coins of different denominations.

The new alloy – 88 percent copper and 12 percent nickel – brought a new color and also a new challenge, both of which have relevance in grading today. The use of nickel in the alloy produced a coin that would wear less quickly than its 100 percent copper predecessors, but the hardness of the copper-nickel planchets caused the dies to wear quickly, contributing to weak strikes.

Set against a plain field, James Barton Longacre's adaptation of Christian Gobrecht's eagle flying left dominates the obverse design with the legend UNITED STATES OF AMERICA about the rim. The date is centered at the bottom. Longacre's agricultural wreath comprising wheat heads, ears of corn in husks, cotton leaves and bolls and tobacco leaves serves as the central reverse design device encircling the ONE CENT denomination legend.

The reverse design was executed so as to give it a high relief on a thick cent planchet. However, the reverse design ultimately led to the design's short life because the deepest areas of the obverse dies were directly opposite the deepest parts of the reverse die, causing metal flow problems in striking that resulted in incomplete strikes. The metal flow-problem proved to be critical and led to the abandonment of the design after just two years of circulation production.

Unlike other copper and copper-alloyed U.S. coins, color attributes are not designated as part of the grade for Flying Eagle cents. However, as with other coins containing copper, Flying Eagle cents over time tend to display the natural toning from the redness of the copper to red-brown to brown. In general, circulated specimens are brown, due to the alloy's interaction with the environment and the oils from human hands that have touched them. Many Uncirculated specimens retain the reddish cast and exhibit enough luster to display a cartwheel effect. Original surfaces on Uncirculated Flying Eagle cents are prized by collectors and often command a premium in the marketplace. Specialists warn that more than 50 percent of the Uncirculated Flying Eagle cents in the marketplace today have been "recolored" or tampered with to the extent that their surfaces can no longer be deemed original.

The greatest grading challenge is being able to distinguish between wear and weak or incomplete strikes on Flying Eagle cents in the About Uncirculated 55 and AU-58 grades and the first level of Uncirculated, Mint State 60.

Wear can be detected best on the design high points, because that's where it appears first.

Grading specialists suggest using incandescent lighting for grading. Also, they suggest inspecting the surface of the coin with your eyes, without magnification, and tilting and rotating the coin, looking for a contrast of luster between the high points and the rest of the coin.

If you detect a contrast of luster between the high points and the rest of the coin, use a loupe or hand-held magnifier of up to a 7-power magnification to inspect for rubbing. Abrasions on the high points drop the grade to circulated.

Not surprisingly, coins with weakness in strike display weakness on the design high points. Weakly struck Flying Eagle cents may appear to have flatness in some areas of the wreath on the reverse. On the obverse, what appears to be wear on Uncirculated specimens may actually be weakness of strike. Check for full luster. The presence of full luster improves the chances you are looking at a weak strike rather than a coin with wear. Die wear can also account for lettering on the obverse appearing to have a washed-out look. Check the fields for evidence of rubbing and discoloration and the tips of the eagle's wings for evidence of wear.

In the Flying Eagle cent map RED is considered Worst (Average x 4), ORANGE is Bad (Average x 2), YELLOW is Average, GREEN is Better (Average x 1/2) and BLUE is Best (Average x 1/4). A mark in the red area is about eight times more serious than if the same mark is in the green area. The worst places on the obverse for a mark or scratch are on the eagle's breast and the date. On the reverse, the ONE CENT denomination legend in the center of the field is considered the worst place for scratches and marks.
(Copyright 1990, HeritageCoins.com)

Design high points for the Flying Eagle cent are shown in red. On the obverse of the Flying Eagle cent, the high points include the center of the eagle's breast, tips of his left wing, the leading feathers of his lower right wing, the feathers just above his claws, and the tips of his tail feathers. On the reverse the design high points are on the center of the bow at the bottom of the wreath, the heads of wheat, the center of the cornhusks, and on the leaves and bolls of cotton on either side.

G-6: Wear is heavy, with design and legend visible, although it can be faint in spots. Obverse: Eagle is outlined, but virtually no detail remains. Rim wear is evident and may be worn into tops of letters in the legend. Reverse: Wreath shows in outline and may exhibit slight detail. Leaves and bow are flat.

VG-8: Design elements are well worn but clear, although they are flat and lack detail. Obverse: Some feather detail visible, usually in the deepest recessed areas and on tip of eagle's right wing. The rim is complete and date and lettering in legend are strong, except in cases of weak strike or die wear. Reverse: Very little detail in the wreath shows. Leaves and the bow are worn and very flat.

F-12: Moderate to heavy wear visible although entire design is clear and bold. Obverse: Some feather details are emerging on eagle's head, breast and tail. Feather details are present on right wing. Ends of wing and tail are clear. Reverse: Some separation of leaves and stalks in wreath are visible but the bow is smooth. Rim is strong on both sides and lettering is clear, except for weak strikes or worn dies.

VF-20: Moderate, even wear evident on both sides. Obverse: Flatness apparent on eagle's breast. More than half of the feather details visible on the eagle's wings and tail feathers are complete. Eagle's head is worn but bold, and his leg is worn smooth. Reverse: Ends of the leaves and the bow are worn smooth.

VF-30: Light, even wear present. Obverse: Spots of wear visible on the eagle's breast and leg. Nearly full detail evident in wing feathers. Some wear present on eagle's head, but it is sharp. Reverse: Some detail emerging on leaves in wreath, although top leaves and bow are very flat from wear.

VF-35: Light, spotty wear present. Obverse: Wear evident in center of eagle's breast and on center of leg. Feather details sharper, with wear pronounced on design high points. Reverse: Details emerging on wheat heads and leaves in lower wreath, although wear is heavy on top portion of wreath.

EF-40: Light wear evident on design high points. Obverse: Details on eagle's wings and tail feathers are plain. Wear visible on high points of breast, wing tips, head and leg. Reverse: Wear evident on high points of leaves and bow in the wreath. Details on stalks and husks are emerging.

EF-45: Very light wear noticeable on design high points. Traces of Mint luster may be present. Obverse: Wear detectable on eagle's breast, head and tips of his wings. All feathers are clear. Reverse: High points on the top leaves and the bow display wear. Details on the remainder of the wreath are emerging.

AU-50: Traces of wear detectable on the design high points. Half of the Mint luster is present. Obverse: Traces of wear show on the eagle's head, breast and left wing tip. Fields are often rubbed and may be discolored. Reverse: Traces of wear show on the lower leaves and bow. Upper leaves lack detail.

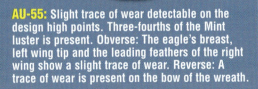

AU-55: Slight trace of wear detectable on the design high points. Three-fourths of the Mint luster is present. Obverse: The eagle's breast, left wing tip and the leading feathers of the right wing show a slight trace of wear. Reverse: A trace of wear is present on the bow of the wreath.

AU-58: Only the slightest trace of wear is visible on the design high points. Nearly full Mint luster is present. Obverse: Look for signs of abrasion on the feathers in the center of the eagle's breast and on the tips of the eagle's wings. Reverse: Check leaves in lower portions of wreath for signs of abrasion. No major detracting contact marks are present and the coin has attractive eye appeal.

MS-60: Strictly Uncirculated with no traces of wear on the design high points. May have heavy contact marks on the eagle and in the field on the obverse. Marks may be present on the wreath, on the denomination in the center and in the field of the reverse. Rim nicks may be present. Mint luster may be dull and unattractive. Color may be dull or dark and coin may contain spots.

MS-61: Strictly Uncirculated with no traces of wear on the design high points. Mint luster may be diminished and surfaces may display large and small contact marks and small hairline scratches. Small rim nicks may be present. Eye appeal is somewhat unattractive and spots may appear on the surface.

MS-62: Strictly Uncirculated with no traces of wear on the design high points. Mint luster may be slightly impaired, but overall eye appeal is generally acceptable. Many small contact marks and a few, scattered heavy contact marks may be present in the prime and secondary focal areas.

MS-63: Strictly Uncirculated with no traces of wear on the design high points. Overall the coin is attractive and has good eye appeal although the Mint luster may be slightly impaired. Some distracting contact marks and hairline scratches may be in prime focal areas.

MS-64: Strictly Uncirculated with no traces of wear on the design high points. Average original Mint luster must be present. Cartwheel effect noticeable. Some light marks may be scattered on the surfaces with a few in the prime focal areas. Overall eye appeal is pleasing.

MS-65: Strictly Uncirculated with no traces of wear on the design high points. Full, original Mint luster must be present, with pleasing cartwheel effect. Light, scattered marks are permitted but no major, distracting marks allowed in prime focal areas. Very pleasing eye appeal.

MS-66: Strictly Uncirculated with no traces of wear on the design high points. Above average, original Mint luster must be present with vibrant cartwheel effect. Several small contact marks permitted, a few of which may be in prime focal areas. Eye appeal is rated at above average.

Indian Head Cent

The first Indian Head cents, produced from 1859 through 1864, are made of 88 percent copper and 12 percent nickel. Because of their brilliant light golden color they were sometimes referred to as "white cents." Depending on the degree of oxidation of the copper, the copper-nickel alloy tones to a medium golden brown.

Continued striking problems with the copper-nickel alloy prompted the U.S. Mint in 1864 to change the metallic content of the Indian Head cent to 95 percent copper and 5 percent tin and zinc, an alloy commonly called bronze.

U.S. Mint Chief Engraver James Barton Longacre designed all versions of the coin. Researcher and specialist Richard Snow maintains that the most accurate description of Longacre's design would be "Liberty with Indian headdress," pointing out that the facial features are Caucasian – believed developed in part from sketches of the chief engraver's daughter, Sarah, at a young age. Longacre wrote that the headdress was inspired by drawings of members of the Chippewa nation in the Lake Superior area. The one-year 1859 reverse features a laurel wreath. The reverse was changed to an oak wreath with a shield at the top in 1860.

Our discussion of grading Indian Head cents concentrates on the bronze issues from 1864 through 1909. Because bronze is softer than the copper-nickel alloy, wear on the design differs. The higher copper content in the bronze issues creates a greater color range from red to red-brown to brown.

Since copper is among the most chemically active of all coinage metals, coins made of high percentages of copper are the most susceptible to change and damage. With bronze coins, surface preservation and eye appeal are key grading components.

When bronze Indian Head cents were first struck they emerged from the dies with a brilliant red-orange surface. This is the color collectors call "red" and abbreviate as RD or R. Exposure to the atmosphere induces oxidization, which produces change in color. The color change can take place slowly or rapidly, depending on the environment in which the coin resides. This mid-range is known as "red and brown" and abbreviated RB. Often specialists denote percentages of red remaining, such as 90 percent, 50 percent, 30 percent and 10 percent.

Over time, especially if exposed to actively circulating air or placed into contact with materials containing sulfur (most paper and cardboard albums), the surfaces of Indian Head cents gradually turn brown. When no trace of red is detectable, the color is described as brown, abbreviated BN or B.

Color on Mint State coins is viewed independent of other factors evaluated for grade. But grade and color are used in determining value. In general, Indian Head cents with full Mint red brilliance are more valuable than red-brown cents and red-brown cents are more valuable than brown pieces.

Mint State Indian Head cents are just as they were struck by the press at the Mint. If a coin has not been circulated, it cannot exhibit evidence of wear. However, a Mint State Indian Head cent can have imperfections and it can be weakly struck and lack details.

As with all U.S. coins series, the mastery of grading Indian Head cents, especially the Mint State range, requires an understanding of and knowledge about what the perfect Indian Head cent would be for each year of issue.

While some specialists aspire to own the highest level of preservation possible for each year and each Mint mark, many collectors are happy to collect at an affordable grade level. In general, collectors strive for uniformity in color when building a collection, select a particular circulated grade and attempt to find all dates and Mint marks in that grade.

Spotting is a particular problem with copper coins and Indian Head cents are not exempt. Frequently the differences in the various Mint State Indian Head cents hinges on the number of spots or slight discolorations present.

In the Indian Head cent map RED is considered Worst (Average x 4), ORANGE is Bad (Average x 2), YELLOW is Average, GREEN is Better (Average x 1/2) and BLUE is Best (Average x 1/4). A mark in the red area is about eight times more serious than if the same mark is in the green area. The worst places on the obverse for a mark or scratch are on the Indian's face and the date. On the reverse, the worst places for scratches and marks are on the shield and the ONE CENT denomination legend in the center of the design. (Copyright 1990, HeritageCoins.com.)

Wear is detected first on the high points of the coin's design, which are highlighted in red. On the obverse of the Indian Head cent, high points are on the Indian's cheek, the hair above the ear and the lowest hair curl just behind the ribbon. On the reverse, the high points are located on the knot of the bow, the acorns in the middle of the wreath and on the outside edges of the leaves. (Copyright 1990, HeritageCoins.com.)

FR-2: Nearly all design details are worn away. Obverse: Head is outlined, lettering in legends is incomplete. Reverse: Rim is worn into the wreath. Lettering in legends is weak and partially missing.

AG-3: Design details outlined, but heavily worn. Obverse: Most of lettering in legends and date are worn but readable. Reverse: Bow is merged with the wreath; the rim is worn into the field. Central lettering is worn but readable.

G-4: Heavily worn. Obverse: Head is outlined, but no fine detail is present. Legend and date are weak but readable. Rim may be worn into tops of lettering in legends. Reverse: Wreath is completely outlined, but worn flat. Bow merges with wreath. Rim may be incomplete in spots.

G-6: Heavily worn, but more detail is present on both obverse and reverse. Denticles show completely on both sides, although some areas may show extensive wear.

VG-8: Design is clear, but flat and well worn. Obverse: Outline of feather ends smooth, but shows. Legend and date are visible. At least three letters of LIBERTY show – any combination of two full letters and parts of two others sufficient. Reverse: Top of wreath is worn smooth, although slight detail is visible. Bow and ribbon are mostly worn flat.

VG-10: Design is clear but worn. Obverse: More detail on head is visible and more detail evident in feathers of headdress. Reverse: Rim is complete. Oak leaf shows recessed detail, although bow and ribbon are worn mostly flat.

F-12: Entire design is clear and bold, although heavy wear is present. Obverse: At least a quarter of details show in hair. Ribbon is worn smooth. No letters are missing in LIBERTY, although some may not be distinct due to weak strike. Lower edge of headband is worn in places. Reverse: Some details are visible in wreath and bow. Tops of leaves are worn smooth and many appear to blend.

F-15: Entire design is clear and bold, with evidence of moderate wear. Obverse. Details of hair are bolder, although only deepest detail shows. LIBERTY is clear and distinct, although some letters may appear weakly struck. Reverse: Leaves in wreath are flat and some blend.

VF-20: All major design features are sharp, although moderate even wear is present. Obverse: Headdress shows good amount of flatness. About half of details show in hair and on ribbon. Head is slightly worn, but bold. Reverse: Lower edge of ribbon around the arrows is completely blended.

VF-30: All major design elements are sharp and light, even wear is present. Obverse: Small flat spots of wear are detectible on tips of feathers, ribbon and ends of hair. At least half of hair details present. May be slightly worn, but all letters of LIBERTY are sharp. Lower ribbon end and lower hair curl are joined. Reverse: Almost full detail shows on leaves and bow.

EF-40: Light wear appears on highest points of design. Obverse: Feathers are well defined. LIBERTY is bold. Wear evident on hair above ear, curl to the right of the ribbon and on the end of the ribbon. Most of diamond design on lower ribbon shows. Reverse: Leaves and bow exhibit wear on high points.

EF-45: Very light wear appears only on highest design points. Obverse: Wear shows on hair above ear, curl to right of ribbon and on the ribbon's end. All diamonds are visible on the lower ribbon and a trace of Mint luster may show. Reverse: Leaves and bow show light wear on high points.

AU-50: Trace of wear is visible on highest points. Half of original Mint luster is present in protected areas of the fields. Obverse: Traces of wear are detectable on the hair above ear and curl to the right of the ribbon. Reverse: Traces of wear are present on the leaves and knot of bow.

AU-55: Small trace of wear detectable on highest points of design elements. Three-fourths of Mint luster remains. Obverse: Trace of wear shows on hair above the ear. Reverse: Trace of wear evident on knot of bow.

MS-63RB: Uncirculated with attractive Mint luster. May have from five to 10 marks on each side and from one to four small spots per side. No large spots are permitted. Traces of red and brown vary.

MS-64RB: Uncirculated with average to full Mint luster. No more than four small marks permitted on each side. No small spots permitted, although a few minute spots may be present. Must have good eye appeal. Traces of red and brown are apparent.

MS-64RD: Uncirculated with average to full Mint luster. No more than four small marks permitted on each side. No small spots permitted, although a few minute spots may be present. Must have good eye appeal. No trace of brown evident.

MS-65RB: Uncirculated with only a few small marks permitted. No spots permitted. Eye appeal must be exceptional. Traces of red and brown evident.

MS-65RD: Uncirculated with only a few small marks permitted. No spots permitted. Eye appeal must be exceptional. No trace of brown permitted.

MS-66RB: Uncirculated. No marks or spots permitted. Has exceptional eye appeal. Traces of red and brown evident.

MS-66RD: Uncirculated. No marks or spots permitted. Has exceptional eye appeal. No trace of brown permitted.

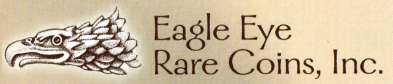

Lincoln Cent

Color must be considered when grading Lincoln cents because color is an important component of grading copper coins.

Since the United States Mint began producing Lincoln cents in 1909, it has used three different copper alloys and one metallic composition without any copper.

From 1909 to 1942, the composition of the Lincoln cent was 95 percent copper, 5 percent zinc and tin. During the World War II years, change was frequent: 1942 – 95 percent copper, 5 percent zinc; 1943 – zinc-coated steel; 1944 to 1946 – 95 percent copper, 5 percent zinc. After the war in 1947, the coin's metallic composition stabilized, returning to the pre-war 95 percent copper and 5 percent zinc and tin and remained until 1962, when tin was dropped again. For the 20-year period 1962 to 1982 the composition was 95 percent copper and 5 percent zinc. Rising costs of copper forced a change in the early 1980s. In 1982 zinc became the primary metal, with the planchet being 97.5 percent zinc and 2.5 percent copper. By weight the coin is 99.2 percent zinc and 0.8 percent copper. The coin retains its copper look because the zinc core is coated with the thin layer of copper.

Thus any collection of Lincoln cents, regardless of grade, is likely to exhibit colors ranging from brown to red-brown to red for the copper alloys and different hues of a dull silver color for the zinc-coated steel cents struck in 1943.

Since copper is among the most chemically active of all coinage metals, coins made of copper are the most susceptible to change and damage. With copper coins, surface preservation and eye appeal are key grading components. In general, Lincoln cents with full Mint brilliance are more valuable than red-brown cents, and red-browns are more valuable than brown pieces.

Because the coloration of a Lincoln cent can be an important factor in determining its grade and ultimately its value, notation of color is frequently used in its description.

When copper alloy Lincoln cents are first struck they emerge from the dies with a brilliant red-orange surface. This is the color collectors call "red." However, once a Lincoln cent is exposed to the atmosphere it immediately begins to oxidize.

Over time, especially if exposed to actively circulating air or placed into contact with materials containing sulfur (most paper and cardboard albums), the surfaces of Lincoln cents will gradually turn brown.

As with all U.S. coins series, the mastery of grading Lincoln cents, especially the Mint State range, requires an understanding of and knowledge about what the perfect Lincoln cent would be for each year of issue.

Victor David Brenner's right-facing bust portrait of Abraham Lincoln graces the obverse. For the first 50 years of issue, heads of wheat embraced the denomination legend on the reverse. In 1959, to honor the 150th anniversary of Lincoln's birth, the reverse was changed to Chief Engraver Frank Gasparro's sculpture of the Lincoln Memorial.

While some specialists aspire to own the highest level of preservation possible for each year and each Mint mark, many collectors are happy to collect from pocket change and take on the challenge of finding the early Lincoln cents, especially those made from 1909 to 1940 that occasionally re-enter circulation from old hoards. In general, they strive for uniformity in color when building a collection and select a particular circulated grade and attempt to find all dates and Mint marks in that grade. For example, one may decide to collect Extremely Fine 45 Lincoln cents red-brown in color. That could be quite a challenge, because the first 20 years of issue are tough to locate, unless one is lucky enough to find hoards, bank bags or early rolls.

Spotting is a particular problem with Lincoln cents. Frequently the differences in the various Mint State Lincoln cents hinge on the number of spots or slight discolorations present.

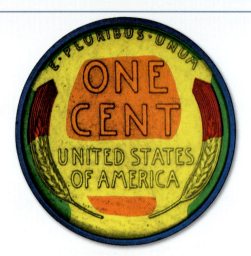

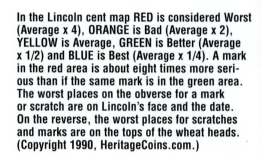

In the Lincoln cent map RED is considered Worst (Average x 4), ORANGE is Bad (Average x 2), YELLOW is Average, GREEN is Better (Average x 1/2) and BLUE is Best (Average x 1/4). A mark in the red area is about eight times more serious than if the same mark is in the green area. The worst places on the obverse for a mark or scratch are on Lincoln's face and the date. On the reverse, the worst places for scratches and marks are on the tops of the wheat heads. (Copyright 1990, HeritageCoins.com.)

Design high points on the obverse and reverse of the Lincoln cent are highlighted in red. The highest points on the obverse are on Lincoln's cheekbone and jawline. High points on the reverse are in the center of the wheat stalks on both sides of the design. (Copyright 1990, HeritageCoins.com.)

Copper Colors

Lincoln cents, when first struck, exhibit a brilliant red-orange surface. Copper coins that retain the red coloration are highly prized by collectors and the color is noted as a factor of the grade. At left, a Mint State 64 red 1957-D Lincoln cent displays brilliant color. As copper oxidizes and reacts with elements in the environment its color will change to brown. The Mint State 1957-D Lincoln cent in the middle photo is an example of a red-brown coloration. The 1951 specimen at right displays the full brown color.

G- 4: Entire coin heavily worn with very few details evident. The legend and date are visible but weak. On the reverse the wheat stalks are worn flat but are completely outlined. Some grains are visible.

VG-8: Overall obverse design is clear, but lacks details due to wear. Outline of hair present, but most details are not. Cheek and jaw are smooth. Just over half of Lincoln's bow tie is evident and the legends and date are clear. On the reverse, some of the wheat details are visible and about half of lines at the top remain.

F-12: Entire design is clear and bold but moderate to heavy even wear is present. Some details visible in the hair, but cheek and jaw are worn smoothly. On reverse, most details show in the wheat stalks. Top lines are worn and separated.

VF-20: Almost all details still present on hair and face although head shows considerable flatness. Ear and bow tie are bold but worn. On reverse wheat stalk lines are worn but no weak spots are visible.

VF-30: All major features are sharp although light to moderate wear shows. Wear on cheek and jaw appears flat, details are still evident in hair. Bow tie and ear clear but slightly worn. On reverse full details of wheat stalks are present, although they are lightly worn.

EF-45: On the obverse slight wear is evident on hair above the ear, cheek and jaw. On the reverse, the high points of wheat stalks are lightly worn and each line is clearly defined. Half of the Mint luster is present.

AU-50: Traces of wear show on the cheek and jaw on the obverse. Wear shows on reverse wheat stalks. At least 75 percent of the Mint luster is present.

AU-55: A trace of wear is visible on the highest point of Lincoln's jaw. A trace of wear shows on the top of the wheat stalks on the reverse. Virtually all of the Mint luster is present.

AU-58: Some signs of abrasion are evident on high points of cheek and jaw as well. Tips of wheat stalks on the reverse also exhibit some signs of abrasion.

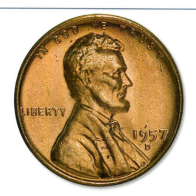

MS-63 Red: No trace of wear is visible and exhibits attractive Mint luster. Has noticeable detracting contact marks or minor blemishes.

MS-64 Red: No trace of wear is evident and exhibits average Mint luster. Attractive overall quality with pleasing eye appeal. May have small number of contact marks.

MS-65 Red: No wear is present and exhibits full Mint luster. A few minor nicks or marks may be visible.

Liberty Head 5 Cents

The Liberty Head 5-cent coin is one of the easier small denomination coins in the U.S. coin series to grade. Although the diameter is only 21.21 millimeters (0.84 inch), the large portrait and uncluttered field render it less of a grading challenge than busier designs on coins of smaller physical size.

Chief Engraver Charles E. Barber, when ordered to create a new look to replace the Shield design on the relatively new 5-cent denomination, returned to the classical allegorical depiction of Liberty as a female.

On first blush, one may think that Barber's head of Liberty is a striking representation of a stylish young woman of the Victorian 1880s. But numismatic art historian Cornelius Vermule notes in *Numismatic Art in America* that Barber's Liberty is "modeled almost verbatim from a Greco-Roman head of Juno," which he points out was well known to engravers at the Philadelphia Mint because a restyling of the famous sculpture was on display at the time at the Philadelphia Academy of Arts.

Barber Americanized his version of the famous sculpture. Liberty's left-facing portrait dominates the obverse. Her long, wavy hair is gently pulled back into a small chignon, with one curl dangling at the nape of her neck. She wears a tiara boldly emblazoned with the word LIBERTY. On the left side, and behind the tiara she wears a small bouquet made from a stalk of cotton bearing three bolls and leaves and two prominent heads of wheat rising at the top. Thirteen six-pointed stars, raised and sculptured with detailed rays, surround Liberty's portrait. The dentiled border features rounded beads. The date is situated below Liberty's neck.

On the reverse Barber featured a large Roman numeral V, meant to covey the denomination, in the center, surrounded by a harvest wreath symbolizing America's bounty. A bow at the bottom binds ears of corn in the husks to stalks of cotton with bolls and stalks with wheat heads on both sides of the open wreath.

The legend E PLURIBUS UNUM is centered below the wreath in the first 1883 reverse, with the legend UNITED STATES OF AMERICA encircling the design on the outside. When the denomination CENTS was added later in 1883 to the reverse, Barber placed a smaller E PLURIBUS UNUM over the top of the wreath and added CENTS below the wreath with dots separating the denomination from the same-sized legend UNITED STATES OF AMERICA.

The edge is plain.

In the Liberty Head 5-cent coin series, strike plays a prominent role. The 75 percent copper, 25 percent nickel composition was relatively new to the U.S. Mint in the early 1880s. Nickel alloy is hard, which diminishes circulation wear, but it was also more difficult to strike, resulting in weak strikes. Graders will often denote "well struck" pieces to recognize strike quality when weaker strikes are typical for the date. The "fully struck" designation is prized, especially in 5-cent coins struck before 1902. Striking quality improved after the third Philadelphia Mint opened in 1902.

Gloria Peters and Cynthia Mohon in their definitive reference, *The Complete Guide to Shield & Liberty Head Nickels,* note that a number of factors affected the quality of nickels minted from 1866 to 1912. In addition to a primitive manufacturing process, the sources of nickel varied, resulting in differences in planchet quality. Other factors researchers Peters and Mohon cite include impure alloy (obtained from melted damaged and noncurrent coins) contaminating new alloy and producing laminations on the planchets. In addition, the nickel alloy's hardness shortened die life. The result of these and other manufacturing problems is that, today, problem-free, fully struck Liberty Head 5-cent coins command a premium in the marketplace.

One of the most important grading decisions is determining whether Liberty Head 5-cent coins exhibit wear.

To detect wear, examine the high points of the design.

In the Liberty Head 5-cent map RED is considered Worst (Average x 4), ORANGE is Bad (Average x 2), YELLOW is Average, GREEN is Better (Average x 1/2) and BLUE is Best (Average x 1/4). A mark in the red area is about eight times more serious than if the same mark is in the green area. The worst places on the obverse for a mark or scratch are on Liberty's face and the date. On the reverse, the worst places for scratches and marks are on the V in the center of the design. (Copyright 2005, HeritageCoins.com)

Wear is detected first on the high points of the coin's design, which are highlighted in red. Liberty Head 5-cent design high points on the obverse include Liberty's full cheek and the cascading wave of hair covering her temple and above to the bottom of the tiara she is wearing. On the reverse the high points are on the top cotton boll and on the wheat stalk leaves and heads on both sides of the top of the open wreath. (Copyright 1990, HeritageCoins.com)

P-1: Design type is identifiable, but both obverse and reverse are so worn that only portions of the legends or inscriptions are legible. Obverse: Liberty's portrait is in outline and identifiable; full date may not be readable. Reverse: Enough of wreath is visible to identify the denomination, although full V is not required.

FR-2: Design type is identifiable, although both obverse and reverse are worn smooth. Obverse: Liberty's portrait is in outline and identifiable; full date is readable. Reverse: Wreath partially visible and V identifying the denomination is fully identifiable.

AG-3: Design elements are in outline, with parts of date and legends worn smooth. Obverse: Liberty's head is in outline with nearly all details worn away. Date is readable, but worn. Reverse: Entire design partially worn away.

G-4: Heavy wear evident. Liberty Head design and legends visible but may be faint in spots. Obverse: Entire design is well worn, but all stars and date are visible. Reverse: Wreath is worn flat. Legend and motto are worn but readable.

G-6: Heavily worn, but all design elements are identifiable. Obverse: Some details on Liberty's head are beginning to emerge, such as her eye and location of her ear. Stars are clear and the date is bolder. Reverse: Wreath shows in bold outline. Legends are readable and bolder.

VG-8: Design is clear, but flat and lacks details. Obverse: Bottom edge of tiara is worn smooth, as are most hair details. At least three letters in LIBERTY are readable. The rim is complete. Reverse: Wreath is clearly visible; rim is complete. Some letters in the motto may be weak.

VG-10: Design is clearer and bolder, although worn. Obverse: Details of hair on forehead and temple area are worn smooth, but beginning to emerge on the back part of Liberty's head. Stars and date are bolder. Reverse: Details of wreath beginning to emerge, although some letters in motto may be weak. The V in center of the design is strong.

F-12: Entire design is clear and bold, although heavy wear is evident. Obverse: Some details show in hair and wave at the top of Liberty's head. All letters of LIBERTY in tiara are visible. Reverse: Some details in wreath visible. Motto letters are worn but clear.

F-15: Moderate wear is evident but entirety of both Liberty's head and wreath is clear and bold. Obverse: More details show in Liberty's hair, and LIBERTY legend on her tiara is stronger. Design details are strong in the wreath and letters in motto are bolder.

VF-20: Moderate, even wear present, but all major features are sharp. Obverse: More than half the details visible on hair and curls. Liberty's head is worn but appears bold. Every letter on the tiara is visible. Reverse: Leaves in the wreath are worn but some of the ribs are visible. Most of the details in the wreath are clear, unless the coin is weakly struck.

VF-30: Light, even wear evident. All major features are sharp. Obverse: Three-fourths of the hair details are visible. The letters in LIBERTY are full and bold. Reverse: Leaves in the wreath are worn but some of the ribs are visible. Some of the lines in the ears of corn are clear, unless the coin is weakly struck.

EF-40: Light wear detectable on design high points. Obverse: Wear evident on Liberty's hair from her forehead to the ear and shows on her cheek and on hair curls. Reverse: Wheat heads and first cotton bolls on each side of wreath exhibit wear, but lines are clearly defined. Corn shows some wear.

EF-45: Very light wear shows on design high points. Obverse: Slight wear evident on Liberty's hair from forehead to ear. Reverse: Slight wear on wheat heads and top cotton bolls. Lines in ears of corn clearly defined. Traces of Mint luster may be present.

AU-50: Traces of wear evident on design high points: Obverse: Traces of wear show on Liberty's hair left of her ear and on her forehead. Reverse: Traces of wear show on the wheat heads, top cotton bolls and ears of corn. Mint luster partially present.

AU-55: Slight traces of wear present. Obverse: Slight trace of wear shows on the highest points of hair to the left of Liberty's ear. Reverse: A trace of wear is present on the ears of corn at the bottom part of the wreath. Half of the Mint luster is present.

AU-58: Very slightest trace of wear detectable on design high points. Obverse: Check high points of Liberty's hair on her forehead and to the left of her ear for signs of abrasion. Reverse: Slightest abrasion may be detected on first ear of corn to the right of the ribbon at the bottom of the wreath.

MS-60: Strictly Uncirculated. No trace of wear permitted. Mint luster may be unattractive, dull or washed out. May have many large detracting contact marks or damage spots. May have heavy concentration of hairline scratches or scuff marks. Rim nicks may be present. Eye appeal is generally poor.

MS-62: Strictly Uncirculated. Mint luster may be dull. Clusters of small contact marks and a few heavy marks or nicks may be in prime focal areas. Hairline scratches may be very noticeable. Strike, rim and planchet quality may be below average. Overall eye appeal is generally acceptable.

MS-63: Strictly Uncirculated. Mint luster may be slightly impaired. Many small contact marks and a few scattered heavy marks may be seen. Small hairlines, visible without magnification, are permitted. Several detracting scuff marks or defects may be present on the design devices or in the fields. The general quality is about average, but overall the coin has attractive eye appeal.

MS-64: Strictly Uncirculated. Exhibits average luster and strike. Several small contact marks in groups, as well as one or two moderately heavy marks, are permitted. One or two small patches of hairlines may show under low magnification. Noticeable light scuff marks or defects permitted on the design devices or in the fields. Exhibits overall pleasing eye appeal.

MS-65: Strictly Uncirculated. Attractive high quality of luster is present. Coin is well struck for the date and Mint mark. A few scattered small contact marks or two larger marks are permitted. One or two small patches of hairlines may show under magnification. Light scuff marks may show on design high points. Overall quality must be above average and the eye appeal should be very pleasing.

Indian Head 5 Cents

Hunting "Buffalos" is an adventure when you're in coin country.

As you scout the territory, you quickly learn that strike plays an important role in the value and desirability of many dates and Mint marks of Indian Head 5-cent coins issued from 1913 to 1938.

It's important to understand the terrain. All Indian Head 5-cent coins, commonly referred to as "Buffalo nickels," are made of 75 percent copper and 25 percent nickel. This particular copper-nickel alloy, while durable, is a hard metal and presents striking problems – especially when an extra-high relief design is employed.

James Earle Fraser's Indian head on the obverse and bison on the reverse are among the highest relief designs ever used on a low-denomination U.S. circulating coin. The Indian Head portrait, facing right, dominates the obverse. Since the portrait occupies most of the coin's canvas, there is a very small field on the right side of the obverse. A left facing, full-figure male bison dominates the reverse, again leaving very little space in the field of the coin.

The powerful design elements are stunning and the coin is a collector favorite, but when grading, one must be aware of what constitutes a "normal" strike for the date and Mint mark.

Specialist David Lange, in the second edition of his book, *The Complete Guide to Buffalo Nickels*, notes: "The Buffalo nickel series is one of the more challenging ones to grade, due to a great variation in the quality of strike. High-grade coins of the Denver and San Francisco Mints may often seem to be well worn, yet the presence of Mint luster dispels this illusion. This phenomenon is particularly evident on Branch Mint coins dated 1917 to 1926."

The weakly struck coins lack design details, even on Uncirculated examples. Because of the prevalence of weak strikes, it is helpful to keep the following years and Mint marks in mind: 1913-S (both design subtypes), 1917-D and -S, 1918-D and -S, 1919-D and -S, 1920-D and -S, 1921-S, 1923-S, 1924-D and -S, 1925-D and -S, 1926-D and -S, 1927-D and -S, 1928-D and -S, 1929-D, 1931-S, 1934-D, 1935-D and the 1937-D Three-Legged Bison variety.

One of the greatest grading challenges is learning to distinguish between the symptoms of weak striking and legitimate wear.

Specialist Lange explains: "The matter of how to grade and price weakly struck coins remains an ongoing concern. In practice, coins that meet most of the criteria for the assignment of a particular grade will usually receive that grade and may be valued in accordance with current price guides. This is particularly true of dates that are highly in demand but are often found inadequately struck.

Well-struck specimens of the same dates will usually command a premium."

One very important facet of grading Indian Head 5-cent coins, especially for circulated specimens, is the emphasis placed on the visibility of the bison's horn. The amount of horn visible in grades Very Good through Very Fine is the primary factor in determining the coin's value. Collectors should be aware that there are variances, especially in the grade Fine 12.

The first five editions of the American Numismatic Association's *Official ANA Grading Standards for United States Coins* specified that three-fourths of the horn must be present in order to attain the F-12 grade. The new, sixth edition is silent on that specification. Many knowledgeable dealers and collectors accept two-thirds of the horn visible as meeting the requirement for the F-12 grade.

A Guide Book of United States Coins ("Red Book") specifies half of the horn must be present for the Very Good 8 grade, and that in order to attain a Very Fine 20 grade the full horn must show.

Throughout the years of issue, the Indian Head 5-cent coin was the most widely used circulated denomination. With the introduction of the coin board in the mid-1930s, many people began collecting them from pocket change. Thus many have survived in circulated grades. The series is avidly collected today in a wide range of grades.

In the Indian Head/Buffalo 5 cent map RED is considered Worst (Average x 4), ORANGE is Bad (Average x 2), YELLOW is Average, GREEN is Better (Average x 1/2) and BLUE is Best (Average x 1/4). A mark in the red area is about eight times more serious than if the same mark is in the green area. The worst places on the obverse for a mark or scratch are on the Indian's face and the date. On the reverse, the worst places for scratches and marks are on the bison's head and body. (Copyright 1990, HeritageCoins.com.)

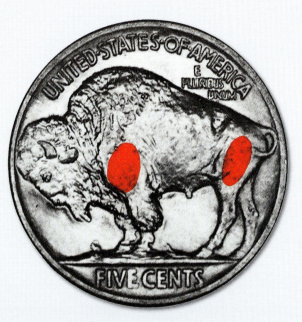

No horn

Half horn

Three-quarters horn

Full horn

Wear is detected first on the high points of the coin's design. On the obverse of the Indian Head, Bison 5-cent coin, the high points are on the Indian's cheek. On the reverse the high points are on the bison's hipbone-flank area and the left shoulder. (Copyright 1990, HeritageCoins.com)

FR-2: Obverse and reverse designs barely discernable. Legends and numerals nearly worn away.

G-4: Design elements and legends heavily worn, but faintly visible in spots. Obverse: Very little detail remaining in central part of design. LIBERTY is weak and merged with the rim. Reverse: Bison is almost flat but is well outlined. Horn does not show. Legend is weak but readable and rim is worn to top of letters.

G-6: Heavy wear on design elements and legends, but detail visible in spots. Obverse: Some detail in central part of design, especially on Indian's hair. Date is readable. LIBERTY present but fades into rim. Reverse: Some detail barely visible on head and front legs of bison. Horn not distinguishable. Legends faint but readable.

VG-8: Overall well worn, but design is clear. Obverse: Indian's hair definable at temple and near cheekbone. Date is clear. LIBERTY merges with rim. Reverse: Some detail present on bison's head. Legends are clear and horn is partially visible, but worn flat.

VG-10: Worn but design is distinguishable. Obverse: More of Indian's hair definable at temple and near cheekbone. Detail beginning to emerge on hair braid. Stronger details in LIBERTY legend. Reverse: Details of bison's beard beginning to emerge and detail on tail discernable. Horn is barely detectable.

F-12: Entire design is clear, although evenly worn. Obverse: Three-quarters of details show in hair and braid. LIBERTY is strong. Reverse: Major details of hair on bison's back are visible. Horn and tail are smooth but are three-quarters visible.

F-15: Designs are clear and bold, although worn. Obverse: Details visible in hairline of forehead and temple area and on hair braid. LIBERTY is bold. Major details on hair on bison's back and front legs are distinct. About 85 percent of smooth horn and tail present.

VF-20: Moderate, even wear on design elements. Obverse: Considerable flatness on hair and cheek, but all details are clear. Feathers exhibit partial detail. Reverse: Hair on bison's head worn. Full horn and tail are visible.

VF-30: Light, even wear on design elements. Obverse: Nearly full detail visible in Indian's hair. Braid and feathers are sharp but worn. Reverse: Bison's head, front legs and hip are worn. Horn is worn, but full. Tail shows.

EF-40: Light wear on the high points of the design devices. Obverse: Some light wear on hair and face, which are bold and well defined. Slight wear visible on lines of the hair braid. Reverse: Horn and end of tail are worn but all details are present.

EF-45: Very light wear on the highest points of the design elements. Obverse: Slight wear detectable on the hair above the braid and there is a trace of wear on the Indian's temple and hair near his cheekbone. Reverse: Light wear noticeable on the high points of the hip and thigh. Bison's horn and tip of the tail are sharp and nearly complete.

AU-50: Traces of Mint luster still show. Obverse: Traces of wear evident on hair. Wear also detectable on left side of forehead and on the cheekbone. Reverse: Wear detectable on the tail and hip. Also, wear evident on the hair above and around the horn.

AU-55: Half of Mint luster still present. Slight traces of wear visible on high points. Obverse: Only trace of wear detectable on high point of cheek. Reverse: Trace of wear shows on the hip.

AU-58: Slightest traces of wear detectable on highest points of design elements. Obverse: Has some signs of abrasion on high points of Indian's cheek. Reverse: May have slight abrasion on hipbone and flank area.

MS-60: No trace of wear evident on high points of designs. May have blemishes and heavy contact marks in all areas. May lack full Mint luster and surfaces may be dull or spotted. May have poor eye appeal.

MS-61: No trace of wear detectable. May have few distracting contact marks in prime focal areas. May lack full Mint luster. Generally unattractive eye appeal.

MS-62: Strictly Uncirculated, no wear. May have some distracting contact marks in prime focal areas. May lack full Mint luster. Eye appeal is generally acceptable.

MS-63: No wear, strictly Uncirculated. May have minor distracting contact marks or minor blemishes. Luster may be original or slightly impaired. Attractive and appealing to the eye.

MS-64: Uncirculated, no wear. May have light, scattered contact marks – a few being in prime focal areas. Mint luster is average, original. Overall appearance is pleasing to the eye.

MS-65: Uncirculated, no traces of wear. May have light nicks or scattered contact marks in prime focal areas. Must have full and original Mint luster. May be unevenly toned or lightly finger-marked. Overall, very pleasing to the eye.

Jefferson 5 Cents

Grading Jefferson 5-cent coins presents some challenges, especially to new collectors.

First, the coin is relatively small in diameter, 21.21 millimeters (.84 of an inch). Thus, for the average person, the design details are more difficult to discern and contact marks and wear may be hard to distinguish without the assistance of a magnifying glass. But too much magnification can be misleading, prompting those new to grading to be overly conservative.

Second, most Jefferson 5-cent coins produced since 1938 are made of an alloy of 75 percent copper and 25 percent nickel. Hence its common name, "nickel." Copper-nickel is a hard alloy and displays a wide range of colors. It also offers a wide range of "looks," especially in the degree of smoothness in the surface of a coin.

Not all "nickels" contain nickel in their alloy. During the war years of 1942 through 1945, the metallic composition of the alloy for the 5-cent denomination was changed to 56 percent copper, 35 percent silver and 9 percent manganese. The coins produced in those years are widely referred to as "Wartime nickels" or "silver nickels."

Bernard A. Nagengast, a Jefferson nickel specialist and author of *The Jefferson Nickel Analyst, Second Edition,* suggests using incandescent lighting for grading Jefferson 5-cent coins. Further, he counsels to inspect the surface of the coins with your eyes, without magnification, tilting and rotating the coin, looking for a contrast of luster between the high points and the rest of the coin.

According to Nagengast, Felix Schlag's design depicting Thomas Jefferson suffers from an inherent flaw: "The highest point on the obverse, Jefferson's hair above his ear, was set exactly opposite the step areas on the reverse." Three things had to be right before a coin could be fully struck up: Die pressure had to be high, the dies had to be adjusted to the optimum distance between their faces when striking a coin, and the planchets had to be of the proper softness through annealing.

The existence of full steps or lack of full steps on the Monticello reverse through the years is a major factor in a fully struck Jefferson 5-cent coin and has led to the use of the term "full steps" and a specialized collecting area. As generally applied, at least five steps must be evident on Monticello to merit the "full-step" designation. The step count includes the porch deck, which is counted as a step. Schlag's design was intended to have six steps. Complete six-step coins produced prior to 1990 command a premium in the marketplace and are designated as "six full steps."

All coinage dies wear due to use. The degree of die wear affects the sharpness of strike. Since copper-nickel is one of the harder coinage alloys, Jefferson 5-cent coins often exhibit weakness of strike due to worn dies. In the Jefferson series, die wear inconsistently differs from year to year and Mint to Mint. The challenge is to know the die characteristics in order to properly grade Jefferson 5-cent coins.

The U.S. Mint has announced that when the Monticello reverse returns to the 5-cent coin in 2006, it will be with the details of Schlag's 1938 design, due to extensive restoration by Mint Sculptor-Engraver John Mercanti.

Schlag's left-facing portrait of Thomas Jefferson's is depicted on the obverse from 1938 through 2004. A new portrait was used in 2005. Monticello, Jefferson's home, occupies the reverse from 1938 through 2003, but was replaced during 2004 and 2005 with designs celebrating the bicentennial of the Corps of Discovery.

Mercanti said in August 2005 that the three-dimensional appearance of the restored design is so vivid that collectors may have to the reexamine how the reverse is graded.

Mercanti used Schlag's original working plaster model from the Mint's archives and the master model for the 2003 reverse (since the technical aspects of the relief of that version were known) to finely hone many of the details of Monticello to make the structure stand out more prominently.

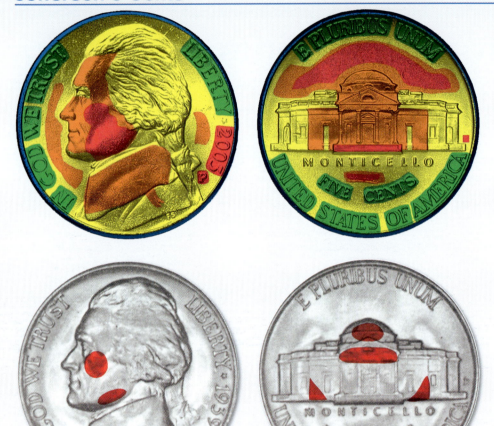

In the Jefferson 5-cent map RED is considered Worst (Average x 4), ORANGE is Bad (Average x 2), YELLOW is Average, GREEN is Better (Average x 1/2) and BLUE is Best (Average x 1/4). A mark in the red area is about eight times more serious than if the same mark is in the green area. The worst places on the obverse for a mark or scratch are on Jefferson's cheekbone and lower jaw, the Mint mark and date. On the reverse, the worst places for scratches and marks are on the steps of Monticello, field above five cents denomination legend and field to right of Monticello. (Copyright 2005, HeritageCoins.com)

High points on the obverse of the Jefferson 5-cent coin are shown in red on cheekbone and lower jaw. On the reverse, design high points are on the dome of Monticello, the triangular roof and beam above the pillars, lower portions of structural walls on the west front. (Copyright 1990, HeritageCoins.com)

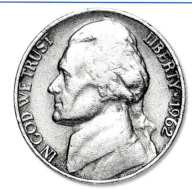

VG-8: Overall the coin is well worn. The design is clear, but flat and lacks details. Obverse: Jefferson's cheek line is visible, but parts are worn smooth; his collar is visible, but weak. Only a few strands of hair show separations. Reverse: Slight detail visible on Monticello. The arch is worn away, pillars barely visible.

F-12: Entire design is clear and bold, but shows evidence of moderate to heavy, even wear. Obverse: Some hair detail visible around Jefferson's face. Cheek line and collar detectable, but weak. Reverse: Some details of Monticello visible behind the pillars. Triangular roof is very smooth.

VF-20: Overall moderate wear, but major features are sharp. Obverse: Cheek line exhibits considerable flatness. More than half of the strands of hair are clear. Partial detail in the collar. Reverse: Pillars are clearly defined but worn. Part of triangular roof is visible.

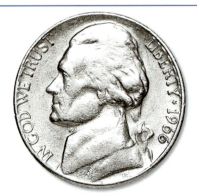

VF-30: Light even wear overall, but all major design elements are sharp. Obverse: Hair is worn, but nearly full details visible. Cheek line and bottom of bust are sharp but worn. Reverse: Most of the pillars show. The triangular roof and beam are worn almost flat.

EF-40: Overall light wear on the highest points of the design elements. Obverse: Hair is well defined and bold, but lightly worn. Cheekbone and bottom of bust exhibit light wear. Reverse: Triangular roof and beam are worn, but all details show.

EF-45: Highest points of design elements evidence very light wear. Obverse: Cheekbone and central portion of hair exhibit slight wear, with a trace of wear at the bottom of the bust. Reverse: High points of triangular roof and beams are worn lightly and traces of Mint luster remain.

AU-50: Small traces of wear visible on highest points of design elements. Obverse: Traces of wear detectable on cheekbone and high points of hair. Reverse: Traces of wear evident on the triangular roof above the pillars and on the beam. Fifty percent of the Mint luster remains.

AU-55: Slight trace of wear on high points. Obverse: Only a trace of wear evident on the cheekbone. Reverse: A trace of wear shows on the beam above the pillars. Seventy-five percent of the Mint luster remains.

AU-58: Very slight traces of wear visible on highest points of design elements. Obverse: Exhibits some signs of abrasion on the cheekbone and high points of hair and collar. Reverse: Abrasion on triangular roof above pillars.

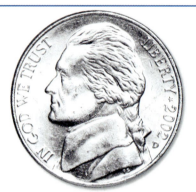
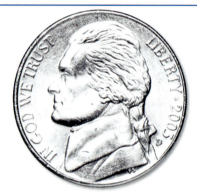

MS-60: There is no trace of wear anywhere on the coin. Both obverse and reverse may have heavy contact marks in all areas. May lack full Mint luster. Surfaces may be spotted and dull. Overall eye appeal is generally poor.

MS-61: May have a few heavy or many light contact marks in prime and secondary focal areas on both the obverse and reverse. Luster often impaired. Overall eye appeal is unattractive.

MS-62: May have some distracting contact marks in prime and secondary focal areas. Luster may be original or impaired. Eye appeal is generally acceptable.

MS-63: May have noticeable detracting contact marks and minor blemishes in prime focal areas. Exhibits attractive Mint luster. Good eye appeal.

MS-64: May have light, scattered contact marks with a few in the prime focal areas. Luster must be average to full and eye appeal generally pleasing.

MS-65: May have light, scattered contact marks, but not in the prime focal areas. Luster must be fully original. Overall eye appeal must be very pleasing.

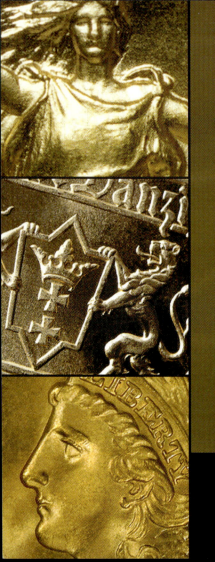

Build lasting wealth.

Collectible rare coins and bullion are not just beautiful pieces of artistry and history, they are also among the most prudent additions to any quality investment portfolio. At Stanford Coins & Bullion, we have one of the most knowledgeable and professional teams in the field of precious metals and rare coins.

Our experts are dedicated to providing each client with the information and individual attention they need to build, manage or enhance their rare coin collection. Our clients have access to research on market trends and coin values, time-tested investment approaches, exclusive liquidation options and unlimited access to our 100 years' combined experience in the industry.

Whether facilitating coin acquisitions or developing an investment strategy, Stanford Coins & Bullion has established a reputation for building lasting client relationships and lasting wealth.

Build to last.

STANFORD COINS & BULLION INC.

3838 North Causeway Blvd., Suite 2020, Metairie, Louisiana 70002
Phone: (504) 833-1690   Fax: (504) 834-9311   Toll-free: 1-800-627-3015

www.StanfordFinancial.com   www.AuctionValues.com   www.StanfordCoins.com
A Member of Stanford Financial Group

Seated Liberty Dime

The Seated Liberty dime can be a challenge to grade. Christian Gobrecht's intricate designs on larger denominations are correspondingly easier to see, but their use on the small diameter (0.61-inch) dime is cause for keeping a magnifier handy. However, specialists suggest using that no more than 2- to 5-power magnification for grading Seated Liberty dimes.

Magnification brings into full view the masterful engraver's creation of Liberty facing left as she sits on a rock or a stone pedestal. She wears a chiton – a long, flowing tunic typically worn by men and women in ancient Greece. The chiton is buttoned at the shoulder and its folds flow naturally. Liberty holds the shield of the United States before her, while resting it firmly in her right hand. Thirteen vertical stripes of the shield alternate in relief and incuse, with horizontal stripes on the top portion of the shield. A scroll bearing the legend LIBERTY is draped across the shield. Liberty holds in her left hand a pole with the Phrygian cap atop, representing freedom from servitude and independence. Liberty rests at ease, with legs outstretched and slightly crossed at the ankles. Yet she remains ready, as indicated by her slight bend forward and a look of vigilance over her shoulder. Her eye is large, as she is the watcher and keeper of a vigilant nation, and her face is slightly raised.

During the 36 years the Seated Liberty design reigned on the dime, it underwent eight major design changes, creating new subtypes each time. It is important to understand the changes because they play a role in grading. The design subtypes are:

1837 through 1838 – No Stars, No Drapery: Obverse has no stars, no legend and no drapery from the elbow of Liberty. Reverse has wreath with ONE DIME in center; long, thin leaves and long-stemmed, closed buds in the wreath; legend UNITED STATES OF AMERICA.

1838 through 1840 – Stars Obverse, No Drapery: Stars added to obverse. Because they were added by hand to each working die, they vary in placement. Reverse same as 1837 through 1838-O.

1840 through 1853 and 1856 through 1860 – Stars Obverse, With Drapery: Obverse has new Liberty sitting up straighter, with drapery under her left elbow, upright shield, stars, and a larger Liberty cap on the pole. Reverse has a new wreath with thicker leaves, open buds.

1853 through 1855 – Stars Obverse, With Arrows: Obverse has arrows added at the date. Reverse same as beginning in 1840.

1860 through 1861 – Legend Obverse, Cereal Reverse Type 1: UNITED STATES OF AMERICA legend replaces stars on the obverse, five vertical lines added above LIBERTY in shield. New Cereal Wreath on reverse with ONE DIME in the center. Left ribbon end is split, and E in ONE is close to the wreath.

1861 through 1873 and 1875 through 1878 – Legend Obverse: Slenderized Liberty, six vertical lines above LIBERTY in the shield.

1873 and 1874 – Legend Obverse, With Arrows: Arrows added at the date on obverse.

1876 through 1891 – Legend Obverse, Cereal Reverse: Obverse Without Arrows, six lines above LIBERTY in the shield. Left ribbon end on reverse is pointed and E in ONE is farther from the wreath.

Seated Liberty dimes were struck at four minting facilities: Philadelphia, New Orleans, Carson City and San Francisco. In general, the Philadelphia Mint strikes tend to be well struck and the strike quality is more consistent than at the Branch Mints. The New Orleans Mint issues are almost always weakly struck. Carson City Mint strikes tend to be well struck but the San Francisco Mint issues vary widely in strike.

Contact marks, tiny hairlines and scuff marks are relatively common on Mint State Seated Liberty dimes. Marks are most critical on Liberty and the open fields on both the obverse and reverse of the coin.

Luster varies widely. Mint State San Francisco and Philadelphia Mint issues commonly exhibit frosty surfaces and New Orleans Mint strikes may have satin to frosty surfaces.

In the Seated Liberty dime map RED is considered Worst (Average x 4), ORANGE is Bad (Average x 2), YELLOW is Average, GREEN is Better (Average x 1/2) and BLUE is Best (Average x 1/4). A mark in the red area is about eight times more serious than if the same mark is in the green area. The worst places on the obverse for a mark or scratch are on Liberty's head, on liberty on shield banner, and the date. On the reverse, the worst places for scratches and marks are in the center field including the one dime denomination legend. (Copyright 1990, HeritageCoins.com)

Design high points on the obverse and the reverse of the Seated Liberty dime are highlighted in red. The highest points on the obverse are Liberty's ear and hair just above it, her breasts, and her right thigh and knee. On the early reverse, high points are on the tips of the leaves, top of the bow and knot of the bow. On the later reverse, high points are on the lower leaves on the left and right sides of the cereal wreath. (Copyright 1990, HeritageCoins.com)

AG-3: Overall design is outlined; parts of legend and date worn smooth. Obverse: Nearly all details worn away but Liberty is outlined. Date is readable but may be very weak. Stars are merging into rim. Reverse: Virtually entire design partially worn away.

G-4: Heavy wear on entire design. Legends visible but may be faint in spots. Obverse: Liberty is outlined but little detail remains. Most of the rim shows. Stars and date are visible. LIBERTY legend worn away. Reverse: Outlined wreath is worn flat. Most letters in legends readable and most of rim shows.

G-6: Design well worn, but some details are beginning to emerge: Obverse: Outline of shield emerging, some details of folds in Liberty's gown distinguishable. Rims and stars are complete. Reverse: Rim is complete, legends are readable.

VG-8: Design well worn, but more details are emerging. Obverse: Entire shield is weak but at least three letters in LIBERTY are readable. Most details of Liberty's gown are worn smooth, but some folds around knees and legs visible. Reverse: Only small amount of detail on wreath shows. Parts of bow very weak.

VG-10: Heavy wear still apparent, but entire design clear and bold. Obverse: Details beginning to emerge of Liberty's face, folds on her gown and drapery. More letters of LIBERTY legend readable. Reverse: All letters of legends strong and readable, wreath and bow clearly defined.

F-12: Moderate to heavy, even wear on design devices. Obverse: Details of Liberty's face, hair and the bodice of her gown emerging. Shield is outlined and letters in LIBERTY are weak but readable. Drapery clasp on Liberty's right shoulder worn away. Reverse: Letters in legend worn but clear. Bow is flat but outlined. Some details in upper portions of wreath emerging.

F-15: Moderate, even wear on design devices. More details of Liberty's face, hair and gown emerging. Shield is outlined and letters in LIBERTY on shield are bolder. Drapery clasp on Liberty's right shoulder emerging. Reverse: Letters in legend and denomination bold and clear. Details on bow and wreath are emerging.

VF-20: Moderate to even wear on design devices but all major features sharp. Obverse: Half of details present in Liberty's gown. Wear evident on Liberty's hair, shoulder and legs, but design devices are bold. All letters in LIBERTY readable. Details on Liberty cap emerging. Reverse: Ribbon is worn, but details emerging. Half of details on leaves clear. Wear spots on bottom leaves and upper stalks.

VF-25: Light, even wear on design devices. Obverse: More than half of details present in Liberty's gown. Liberty's hair, shoulder and legs are bolder. All letters in LIBERTY are readable, scroll edge nearly complete. More cap details visible. Reverse: Ribbon details are bolder. Details of corn kernels and wheat heads are visible in wreath.

VF-30: Light, even wear on design devices. Obverse: Wear spots visible on Liberty's shoulder, breast, knee and legs. Details are emerging on Liberty's head. LIBERTY and scroll are complete. Reverse: Most details are visible in leaves of wreath. Most details in ribbon and bow are clear.

VF-35: Light wear on design devices. Obverse: Some wear spots visible on Liberty's shoulder, breast, knee and legs. More details show on Liberty's head. Reverse: Some wear shows on bottom leaves, but most details of leaves, wheat heads and ears of corn are visible. Most ribbon details clear.

EF-40: Light wear on high points of design. Obverse: Wear visible on Liberty's knees, head and shoulder. Wear shows at neckline of Liberty's gown. LIBERTY is complete and edges of scroll are raised. Reverse: All design details are clearly defined, but wear evident on high points of wreath and bow. Traces of luster may be present.

EF-45: Very light wear on design high points. Obverse: Slight wear evident on high points of knees and hair on Liberty's forehead. Drapery displays wear on shoulder and at bustline. LIBERTY is sharp and edges of scroll are raised. Reverse: Wear evident on high points of wreath and bow. Lines in leaves are clearly defined. Some luster is evident.

AU-50: Trace of wear is visible on design high points. Obverse: Traces of wear detectable on Liberty's knees, right shoulder and at edge of hairline. Reverse: Traces of wear evident on bow and tips of leaves. Half of the luster is present.

AU-53: Trace of wear is visible on design high points. Obverse: Traces of wear detectable on Liberty's knees and at edge of hairline. Reverse: Traces of wear evident on bow and tips of leaves. More than half of original Mint luster is present.

AU-55: Slightest trace of wear evident on high points of Liberty's knees. Slight trace of wear evident on bow. Three-fourths of original Mint luster is present.

AU-58: Slightest trace of wear detectable on design high points. Obverse: Some signs of abrasion detectable on high points of Liberty's knees and breast. Reverse: Detectable abrasion on tips of leaves in wreath and on the bow. More than three-fourths of original Mint luster present.

MS-60: Uncirculated. Absolutely no trace of wear permitted. Mint luster may be unattractive, dull or washed out. May have large, detracting contact marks in all areas or damage spots. Rim nicks may be present. May have a patch of or continuous hairline scratches on surfaces. Eye appeal is very poor.

MS-63: Uncirculated. Slight impairment of Mint luster detectable. A few scattered heavy marks and numerous small contact marks permitted. Small hairline scratches visible without magnification. Several scuff marks or detracting defects may be present on design elements or in the fields. General quality of the coin is about average. Overall, the coin is rather attractive.

MS-65: Uncirculated. Mint luster and strike are attractive and of high quality for the date and Mint facility at which coin was struck. A few small and scattered contact marks or two larger marks permitted. One or two small patches of hairline scratches are visible under magnification. Light scuff marks may be detectable on design high points. Quality overall is above average and overall eye appeal is very pleasing.

GRADING POSTERS

These 2-foot by 3-foot posters feature detailed, high-quality enlarged photos of the top 25 collected U.S. coins. Both the obverse and reverse of the graded coins are shown on each poster, enabling collectors to clearly see the differences between grades. Also included on the posters are color-coded wear and contact maps that show where the high points of the design will wear first and where contact marks have the least and greatest impact on the grade. A complete set of 25 different Grading Posters housed in a heavy-duty storage box is also available.

ITEM	DESCRIPTION	RETAIL	AA*
GPSET	25 Posters & Storage Box	$549.99	**$399.99**

TO ORDER CALL 1-800-572-6885
www.amosadvantage.com

POSTERS AVAILABLE

Retail $24.99 ea.   AA* **$19.99** ea.

ITEM	DESCRIPTION
GP01	Large Cents
GP02	Flying Eagle Cents
GP03	Indian Cents
GP04	Lincoln Cents
GP05	Liberty Head Nickels
GP06	Buffalo Nickels
GP07	Jefferson Nickels
GP08	Seated Liberty Dime
GP09	Liberty Head (Mercury) Dimes
GP10	Roosevelt Dimes
GP11	Barber Quarters
GP12	Standing Liberty Quarters
GP13	Washington Quarters
GP14	Statehood Quarters 1999-2005
GP15	Barber Half Dollars
GP16	Walking Liberty Half Dollar
GP17	Franklin Half Dollars
GP18	Kennedy Half Dollars
GP19	Morgan Dollar
GP20	Peace Dollar
GP21	Eisenhower Dollar
GP22	Susan B. Anthony Dollars
GP23	Sacagawea Dollars
GP24	Coronet Head $20 Gold
GP25	Saint-Gaudens $20 Gold

AA* prices apply to paid subscribers of *Coin World* or *Coin Values*.

AMOS ADVANTAGE

Winged Liberty Head Dime

Generally the smaller the coin, the more difficult it is to grade.

The 10-cent coin, known as the dime, has been the smallest diameter U.S. coin in circulation (diameter: 17.91 millimeters or 0.71 inch) for more than a century. Logically it would be in the "harder to grade" column. But that's not necessarily the case with the Winged Liberty Head series, struck from 1916 through 1945.

The ease with which it can be graded is largely attributable to designer Adolph Weinman's full use of the coin's canvas. Although intricate in detail, Weinman's left-facing profile bust of Liberty on the obverse occupies most of the coin's surface, with the remainder apportioned to the field.

Liberty's face is framed by her thickly curled and wavy hair, held in place by the Phrygian cap to which Weinman added a wing. Use of the Phrygian cap (also depicted on earlier U.S. coins) harkens back to an ancient Greek symbol connoting freedom. When queried about the wing, Weinman said he added it to symbolize liberty of thought. The primary design device on the reverse is a Roman symbol known as a fasces. An ax blade, facing left, projects at the top, bound into to a bundle of rods secured by leather straps (bands) wound both horizontally and diagonally. Intertwined with the fasces is an intricately detailed large olive branch.

The fasces was an ancient symbol of power and authority carried by Roman magistrates. Weinman said he used "the motive of the fasces and olive branch to symbolize the strength which lies in unity, while the battle-ax stands for preparedness to defend the Union. The branch of olive is symbolical of our love of peace."

The greatest challenge in grading Winged Liberty Head dimes is being able to distinguish weak strike from wear.

Specialist David W. Lange, writing in *The Complete Guide to Mercury Dimes*, notes that "most dimes coined at the Denver and Philadelphia Mints from 1917 through 1928 will exhibit some areas of weakness. This is commonly seen in the centers of their obverse and reverse or around their peripheries. In particularly bad instances, deficiencies will be found in both locations." Lange also cautions that none of the dimes struck from 1925 through 1945 exhibit the fine details of earlier years. This he attributes to continued use of worn master hubs in the die manufacturing process.

A number of dates tend to be poorly struck, lacking full details, regardless of condition. They include: 1916-D, 1918-S, 1919-S, 1920-S, 1921, 1921-D, 1923-S, 1924-S, 1925-D, 1925-S, 1926-S, 1927-D, 1927-S, 1928-S, 1930-S, 1931-S, 1934 and 1939-S.

One of the most critical strike factors for the Winged Liberty Head dimes is whether on the reverse the horizontal bands binding the fasces are complete. Although the top and lower bands are important, the center bands are crucial to the coin being deemed to have "full bands" or "full split bands." To qualify there can be no interruption in the groove of the bands due to strike or contact marks, planchet problems or any other damage. Although the center bands must be fully separated and exhibit no interruptions, they do not have to be fully rounded. On some coins the bands appear to be flat but the groove is not interrupted. Connectors that some refer to as "bridges" to the depression between the bands disqualify an example from the lofty status of full bands.

The Winged Liberty Head dime is one of the few series in which a feature on the reverse determines value. Two dimes of equal grade, one exhibiting full bands and the other falling short of meeting the qualification, have dramatically differing values in today's market. The full bands dimes bring higher premiums than coins in the same numerical grade lacking the distinction. It pays to look for full split bands in the following date/Mint mark combinations because they are rare: 1917-D, 1918-D, 1918-S, 1919-D, 1919-S, 1931-S, 1935-D, 1939-S and 1945.

In the Winged Liberty Head dime map RED is considered Worst (Average x 4), ORANGE is Bad (Average x 2), YELLOW is Average, GREEN is Better (Average x 1/2) and BLUE is Best (Average x 1/4). A mark in the red area is about eight times more serious than if the same mark is in the green area. The worst places on the obverse for a mark or scratch are on Liberty's face and the date. On the reverse, the worst places for scratches and marks are on the center bands binding the rods and in the field at the base of the olive branch. (Copyright 1990, HeritageCoins.com)

Wear is detected first on the high points of the coin's design, which are highlighted in red. The highest points on the obverse of the Winged Liberty Head dime are on Liberty's cheek and at the ear level on the wing. The highest points on the reverse are on the centers of the diagonal bands binding the rods. (Copyright 1990, HeritageCoins.com)

Bands

When center horizontal bands on the reverse of an Uncirculated Winged Liberty Head dime are filled or only partially separated, the coin does not qualify for Full Bands or Full Split Bands.

Full separation, identified as Full Bands or Full Split Bands, on the center horizontal bands on the reverse make the Winged Liberty Head dime more valuable than an equivalent grade exhibiting filled or partially separated bands.

AG-3: Most design details are outlined, although parts of the date and legends are worn smooth. Obverse: Liberty's head is outlined, but most details are worn away. Date is worn but readable. The LIBERTY legend merges into the rim. Reverse: All of the design is partially worn away. Rim is worn at least halfway into the legend.

G-4: Design details and legends are heavily worn but visible and may be faint in spots. Obverse: Liberty is well worn, as are other design elements; little detail remains. Legend and date are visible but may be weak. The rim is detectable. Reverse: The fasces is completely outlined but is worn nearly flat. The rods and bands are worn smooth.

G-6: Design details and legends heavily worn, but some detail emerging. Obverse: Details on Liberty's hair and the upper portion of the wing beginning to be visible. Legend, motto and date are stronger. Reverse: The fasces is completely outlined and worn, but more detail discernable on olive branch. Legend somewhat stronger.

VG-8: Design is well worn but clear, lacking details. Appears flat. Obverse: Liberty's head is weak, and most details in the wing are worn smooth. The rim is complete. Reverse: Some vertical lines in the fasces visible. The rim is complete.

F-12: Extensive even wear evident, but the entire design is clear and bold. Obverse: Some details show in hair. Wing feathers are partially visible but are weak. Curls and waves in hair nearly worn away. Reverse: Vertical lines in fasces are visible but lack sharpness. Diagonal bands worn but detectable, with one worn smooth at mid-point.

F-15: Moderate, even wear visible on entire design, but design is bolder. Obverse: More details evident in Liberty's hair, and wing feathers are bolder and more detailed. Reverse: Vertical lines in fasces detectable and slightly sharper. More of diagonal bands visible.

VF-20: Moderate even wear on the design, but all major features are sharp. Obverse: Liberty's hair is worn, but some details are visible. Three-fourths of detail present in feathers of wing. Reverse: Wear evident on the two diagonal bands, but most details are visible. All of the vertical lines in the fasces evident. All details in the olive branch are clear.

VF-30: Light even wear on the design and all major features are sharp. Obverse: Some wear shows on Liberty's hair along her face, cheek and neckline. The wing feathers exhibit nearly full detail but are weak. Reverse: Wear shows on the two diagonal bands, but most details are visible. All of the vertical lines are sharp, and all of the details in the olive branch are clear.

EF-40: Light wear evident on the highest points of the design. Obverse: Wear evident on the high points of Liberty's hair and at her neckline and on the wing of her cap. Reverse: High points on the diagonal bands on the fasces exhibit wear, but rod details clearly defined and partially separated. Traces of Mint luster may be present.

EF-45: Very light wear detectable on only the highest points of the design. Obverse: Slight wear shows on high points of Liberty's hairline and on the feathers of the wing. Hair along Liberty's face is sharp and detailed. High points of the diagonal bands binding the fasces are lightly worn. Horizontal band lines are clearly defined but are not fully separated. Part of Mint luster may be present.

AU-55: Traces of wear visible on highest points of the design. Obverse: Trace of wear detectable on hair above Liberty's forehead and in front of her ear. Reverse: Trace of wear shows on the horizontal and diagonal bands binding the fasces. Three-fourths of the Mint luster is present.

AU-58: Some signs of abrasion on the design high points. Obverse: Slightest trace of wear on the high points on Liberty's hair and in front of her ear. Reverse: Slight trace of wear on the middle of two diagonal bands binding the rods of the fasces.

Winged Liberty Head Dime

MS-61: Strictly Uncirculated coin with no trace of wear. May have a few heavy contact marks or many light marks in prime and secondary focal areas. Noticeable patches or continuous hairline scratches are permitted on the surfaces. May lack full Mint luster and surface may be dull, spotted or heavily toned.

MS-63: Strictly Uncirculated coin with no trace of wear. Displays attractive Mint luster but may exhibit distracting contact marks in the prime focal areas and a few scattered or small patches of hairline scratches. Horizontal bands on the reverse may be filled or partially separated.

MS-63B: Strictly Uncirculated coin with no trace of wear. Displays attractive Mint luster but may exhibit distracting contact marks in the prime focal areas and a few scattered or small patches of hairline scratches. Horizontal bands – particularly the middle band – are fully separated.

MS-64: Strictly Uncirculated coin with no trace of wear. May have light, scattered contact marks with a few being in the prime focal areas. May have a few scattered or a small patch of hairline scratches in secondary focal areas. Must exhibit average to full Mint luster and have pleasing eye appeal. Horizontal bands on the reverse may be filled or partially separated.

MS-64B: Strictly Uncirculated coin with no trace of wear. May have light, scattered contact marks with a few being in the prime focal areas. May have a few scattered or a small patch of hairline scratches in secondary focal areas. Must exhibit average to full Mint luster and have pleasing eye appeal. Horizontal bands – particularly the middle band – are fully separated.

MS-65: Strictly Uncirculated coin with no trace of wear. May have light and scattered contact marks but no major distracting marks in prime focal areas. May have a few scattered hairline scratches but not in prime or secondary focal areas. Mint luster must be fully original and have very pleasing eye appeal. Horizontal bands on the reverse may be filled or partially separated.

MS-65B: Strictly Uncirculated coin with no trace of wear. May have light and scattered contact marks but no major distracting marks in prime focal areas. May have a few scattered hairline scratches but not in prime or secondary focal areas. Mint luster must be fully original and have very pleasing eye appeal. Horizontal bands – particularly the middle band – are fully separated.

MS-66: Strictly Uncirculated coin with no trace of wear. May have a few, small contact marks in prime focal area but no hairline scratches visible to the naked eye. Must exhibit above average fully original Mint luster. Eye appeal must be above average. Horizontal bands on the reverse may be filled or partially separated.

MS-66B: Strictly Uncirculated coin with no trace of wear. May have a few, small contact marks in prime focal area but no hairline scratches visible to the naked eye. Must exhibit above average fully original Mint luster. Eye appeal must be above average. Horizontal bands – particularly the middle band – are fully separated.

Roosevelt Dime

The Roosevelt dime is a challenge to grade primarily because of its size. With a diameter of 17.91 millimeters or 0.71 of an inch, it is the smallest U.S. circulating coin. Although its design devices are large and bold on the tiny canvas, inspection for grading purposes will send most collectors reaching for some form of magnification.

The coin was first issued on Jan. 30, 1946, the late president's birthday.

U.S. Mint Chief Engraver John R. Sinnock chose to portray a left-facing portrait of Franklin Delano Roosevelt on the obverse of the new dime.

A flaming torch signifying liberty is the central device on the reverse. An olive branch, with two olive fruits, to the left of the torch, signifies peace. An oak branch bearing two acorns, to the right of the torch, signifies strength and independence.

On the 90 percent silver dimes dated from 1946 through 1964, the Mint mark, when used, is located to the left of the base of the torch on the reverse. Mint marks, when used, were changed to the obverse – above the date – beginning in 1968.

From 1946 through 1955, Roosevelt dimes were struck for circulation at the Philadelphia, Denver and San Francisco Mints, although only the Denver and San Francisco strikes carry Mint marks. From 1956 through 1964, no circulation-strike Roosevelt dimes were struck at the San Francisco Mint.

Although regular issue Roosevelt dimes were struck at the Philadelphia, Denver and San Francisco Mints from 1965 through 1967, no Mint marks appear on them.

Proof versions of the Roosevelt dime were struck at the Philadelphia Mint from 1950 through 1964 and have no Mint mark. Today, sometimes impaired Proofs from the 1950 to 1964 era are included in privately assembled sets of Uncirculated coins because those assembling the set mistake the Proof as an Uncirculated Philadelphia Mint strike without a Mint mark.

Since 1980, the U.S. Mint has been designating coins struck at the Philadelphia Mint with the P Mint mark on circulating denominations above the date.

In 1996, the Mint produced a special 50th anniversary circulation-strike version of the Roosevelt dime at the West Point Mint located in Roosevelt's home state of New York. The 1996-W Roosevelt dime was available only in Uncirculated Mint sets produced and sold during 1996.

Collecting choices differ for Roosevelt dimes. Some collect only the 90 percent silver "early" Roosevelt dimes, while others are inclusive, adding what is known simply as the "clad" Roosevelt dimes – composed of two outer layers of 75 percent copper, 25 percent nickel "silver color" cladding bonded to an inner pure copper core.

Metal composition is important in grading Roosevelt dimes. The softer, 90 percent silver coins are much more susceptible to wear, nicks and scratches than those of the harder clad alloy composition. During the past 40 years, as the Mint has increased mintages for the circulation-strike clad Roosevelt dimes to meet the needs of commerce, it has gradually lowered the relief, reducing the coin's susceptibility to wear. It is possible to find a new Roosevelt dime in circulation with little to no signs of wear, even on the high points of the design. Thus, Roosevelt dimes plucked from circulation for collections tend to be in the About Uncirculated range – AU-50, AU-55 and AU-58.

One fact to remember is that Roosevelt dimes struck at the San Francisco Mint tend to exhibit weakness of strike. Areas to check for weakness of strike include FDR's ear, the hair above his ear and the hair on the top of his head. Weakness is sometimes found on the torch on the reverse. Often in weak strikes, the flame and base of the torch will have a mushy appearance. Other areas of the reverse that may exhibit weakness of strike include the central portion of the torch, leaves in both the olive and oak branches on either side of the torch, and the motto E.PLURIBUS.UNUM.

In the Roosevelt dime map RED is considered Worst (Average x 4), ORANGE is Bad (Average x 2), YELLOW is Average, GREEN is Better (Average x 1/2) and BLUE is Best (Average x 1/4). A mark in the red area is about eight times more serious than if the same mark is in the green area. The worst places on the obverse for a mark or scratch are on Roosevelt's cheek and the date. On the reverse, the lower horizontal bands on the torch are the worst places for scratches and marks. (Copyright 2005, HeritageCoins.com)

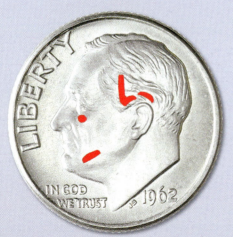

Design high points for the Roosevelt dime are shown in red. Design high points on the obverse of the Roosevelt dime are on the hair above FDR's ear, on the cheekbone, and along the jawbone. High points on the reverse include: the center of flame atop the torch, the top and lower horizontal bands on the torch, center of the lower right leaf of the olive branch cluster to the left of the torch, and the center of the top leaf in the oak branch to the right of the torch.

F-12: Moderate to heavy, even wear on design elements, although entire design is clear and bold. Obverse: Roosevelt's face is worn, but solidly visible. Half of details in his hair are identifiable. Half of inner edge of FDR's ear is worn away. Reverse: Vertical lines of the torch are faintly visible, but horizontal bands are worn smooth. Flame on the torch is nearly worn smooth. Some detail is visible on olive and oak leaves.

VF-20: All major design elements are sharp, but display moderate, even wear. Obverse: Wear evident on FDR's face, but his face is bold. At least three-fourths of the details show in his hair. Some details in his ear are visible. Reverse: Vertical torch lines exhibit wear but are identifiable. Flame is worn but some line detail is emerging. Details on olive and oak leaves are emerging.

VF-30: Light to moderate wear evident on major design elements, but all major features are sharp. Obverse: Spots of wear show on FDR's cheek, chin, ear and hair. Details of hair are almost fully visible, although the lines may appear weak. Reverse: Vertical lines of the torch identifiable and most details of the torch and leaves are clear. Flame exhibits wear but some details are visible.

EF-40: Light wear evident on design elements. Obverse: Wear detectible on the high points of FDR's hair, cheekbone and upper tip of the ear. Reverse: Wear evident on high points of flame, torch and leaves, but all details are clearly defined. A trace of Mint luster may be present.

EF-45: Very light wear visible on design high points. Obverse: Slight wear visible on high points of hair above FDR's ear. The ear is detailed and sharp. Reverse: Light wear detectable on high points of flame. Lines on the torch are clearly defined and fully separated. Part of Mint luster is present.

AU-50: Traces of wear visible on highest points of design elements. Obverse: Traces of wear detectable on hair above FDR's ear. Reverse: Details on flame are sharply defined but traces of wear still visible.

AU-55: Small traces of wear visible on design high points. Obverse: Slight trace of wear visible on the high points of hair above FDR's ear. Reverse: Slight trace of wear detectable on highest points of the flame atop the torch. Three-fourths of Mint luster present.

AU-58: Slightest evidence of wear on highest points of design elements. Obverse: Some signs of abrasion detectable on high points of FDR's cheek and the hair above his ear. Reverse: Some signs of abrasion on tops of leaves and details in flame.

MS-60: Strictly Uncirculated, with no trace of wear. May have heavy contact marks in all areas and a noticeable patch of hairline scratches. Full Mint luster present, but surface may be dull, spotted or toned.

MS-61: Strictly Uncirculated, with no trace of wear. May have a few heavy or numerous light contact marks in the prime or secondary focal areas. May have a noticeable patch or continuous hairline scratches on the surfaces. Small rim nicks, striking or planchet defects may be visible. Mint luster may be diminished or noticeably impaired. Eye appeal is somewhat unattractive.

MS-62: Strictly Uncirculated, with no trace of wear. Clusters of small contact marks may be present over entire surface. A few large contact marks or nicks permitted in prime focal areas. Hairline scratches may be very noticeable. Planchet quality, strike and rim may be noticeably below average. Mint luster may be dull or impaired. Overall eye appeal is generally acceptable.

MS-63: Strictly Uncirculated, with no trace of wear. May have distracting small contact marks in prime focal areas and possibly a few heavy marks. Small hairline scratches are visible without magnification. Mint luster is attractive. General quality is about average. Overall, the coin is rather attractive.

MS-64: Strictly Uncirculated, with no trace of wear. May have light, scattered contact marks, with a few in prime focal areas. May have few scattered hairline scratches or a patch of hairlines in secondary focal areas visible under low magnification. Full, original, average Mint luster is present. Eye appeal is generally pleasing.

MS-65: Strictly Uncirculated, with no trace of wear. The few contact marks permitted are light and scattered. No major distracting contact marks permitted in prime focal areas. One or two small patches of hairline scratches may show under magnification. Mint luster must be fully original and of attractive high quality. Eye appeal is very pleasing.

MS-66: Strictly Uncirculated, with no trace of wear. No more than two or three minor, small contact marks permitted. A few, very light hairline scratches may show under magnification. Must have above average quality of strike. Mint luster must be full and original. Eye appeal must be above average and very pleasing for the date and Mint mark.

Barber Quarter Dollar

Mint Chief Engraver Charles E. Barber's head of Liberty did not win the praise of the artistic community when it first appeared on circulating half dollars, quarter dollars and dimes in 1892. But more than a century later, collectors and graders acknowledge his technical achievement in low relief, which enabled coins that widely circulated for decades to survive with so much of their design elements in full complement.

In 1891 Mint Director Edward O. Leech convinced Congress to approve legislation clarifying Treasury's authority to change coin designs after a design has been in circulation for at least 25 years.

When a compensated design competition failed to attract artists outside government employ, Barber announced that he was the only person capable of rendering designs that would meet the technical and low relief coining requirements of the Mint's equipment.

The Mint's official description of the design states: "On the obverse is a female head, representative of liberty, looking right, expression calm and dignified, with olive wreath around the head and Phrygian cap on back. On a band over front of head the word 'Liberty' and over the head the motto 'In God we trust;' around the medallion are thirteen stars, and under, the date of coinage. On the reverse appears the seal of the United States as adopted 1782, and is thus described: An eagle displayed, charged on the breast with a shield argent, six pallets gules, a chief azure, holding in the dexter claw an olive branch of thirteen leaves; in the sinister claw a sheaf of thirteen arrows; in the beak a scroll with the motto 'E Pluribus Unum,' ensigned above and about the head with thirteen stars."

Art and numismatic historians point out that Barber borrowed heavily from 19th century French coins and medals in developing his "staid, heavy-featured head of Liberty." Cornelius Vermeule, writing in *Numismatic Art in America,* notes: "Of all American coins long in circulation, no series has stood the wearing demands of modern coinage so well as the half dollar, quarter, and dime developed by the Chief Engraver at Philadelphia."

David Lawrence Feigenbaum, writing under the name David Lawrence, provides collectors with an in-depth date and Mint mark study of the series in *The Complete Guide to Barber Quarters* and notes that the Barber quarter dollars are "easy to grade in circulated condition," but cautions that "like many U.S. coins, the strike must be taken into consideration." He especially points to Barber quarter dollars struck at the New Orleans Mint as often being weakly struck and lacking details on Liberty's forehead and the wreath she wears in her hair. On the reverse of New Orleans Mint coins, he suggests looking for weakness of strike "along a vertical path from the right corner of the shield down to the eagle's claw."

He also advises that a hub change in 1900 altered the design enough to affect grading. He notes that Barber quarter dollars from 1892 to 1900 in grades Very Fine to Extremely Fine and sometimes About Uncirculated tend to show more detail over Liberty's forehead than those struck from 1900 to 1916. According to the researcher, it is not unusual for VF coins dated 1892 to 1900 to have a full band under LIBERTY, but the band may not be complete on some coins graded EF on dates from 1900 to 1916. In addition, the later dates (1910 to 1916) tend to exhibit weaker strikes than earlier dates.

In addition, some Barber quarter dollars struck at the Denver Mint were softly struck, particularly on the eagle's left claw and sometimes on the LIBERTY legend on the band. The toughest call in grading these coins is in distinguishing between weak striking and legitimate wear.

Professional graders suggest their best advice in grading Barber quarter dollars is "to grade the entire coin," rather than focusing almost exclusively on the obverse.

In the Barber quarter dollar map RED is considered Worst (Average x 4), ORANGE is Bad (Average x 2), YELLOW is Average, GREEN is Better (Average x 1/2) and BLUE is Best (Average x 1/4). A mark in the red area is about eight times more serious than if the same mark is in the green area. The worst places on the obverse for a mark or scratch are on Liberty's face, which is the focal point of the coin. On the reverse, the eagle's head and neck are the worst places for scratches and marks. (Copyright 2005, HeritageCoins.com)

Design high points on the Barber quarter dollar are highlighted in red. The highest points on the obverse are on Liberty's cheek and the hair just above her forehead. The highest points on the reverse are the eagle's head and neck feathers, tips of both wings and the center tail feathers. (Copyright 1990, HeritageCoins.com)

AG-3: Design is outlined and parts of date and legend are worn smooth. Obverse: Nearly all details are worn away, but head is outlined. Date is readable, but may be partially worn away. Motto is merging into rim. Reverse: Entire design displays heavy wear and legends are merging with rim.

G-4: Heavy wear evident, but design and legend are visible, although they may be faint in some areas. Obverse: Little detail remains because entire design is well worn. LIBERTY is worn away. Motto is weak but readable. Reverse: Eagle is worn flat but is completely outlined. Ribbon is worn smooth. Legends are weak but distinct. Rim worn to tops of letters in legends.

G-6: Rims are complete on both obverse and reverse for most dates. Obverse: Some of detail on Liberty's wreath beginning to show with possibly the beginning of the L in the word LIBERTY. Reverse: Small amounts of detail beginning to show on eagle.

VG-8: Designs are clear but flat and well worn, lacking detail. Obverse: Most details in the face are worn smooth; entire head is weak. First three letters in LIBERTY are emerging. Rim is complete. Reverse: Eagle is well worn but small amounts of detail emerging, such as eagle's eye. Most of the shield is very weak.

VG-10: Wear evident on design details: Obverse: Four to five letters of LIBERTY discernable, although some will be very weak. More detail is present in Liberty's head wreath. Reverse: More detail emerging on eagle's wings, shield and ribbon in beak.

F-12: Moderate to heavy even wear evident but designs are clear and bold. Obverse: Some details show in facial features, hair, and cap. All letters in LIBERTY visible, but may be weak. Upper leaves are outlined, but bottom leaves are worn nearly smooth. Rim is bold and full. Reverse: Half of eagle's feathers are visible, but wear spots evident in center of neck and on the motto and arrows. Vertical shield lines are separated but horizontal lines are merged. Letters in legends are worn, but clear.

F-15: Moderate wear on design devices. Obverse: More details show in hair, facial features, and cap. Most letters in LIBERTY are complete, although bottom of the R may be weak. More detail in leaves present. Reverse: More details on eagle's feathers and arrows present. All of motto is readable. Horizontal lines in shield are distinctive.

VF-20: Moderate, even wear overall, but all major design elements are sharp. Obverse: More than half of details of leaves evident. Wear visible on hair and ribbon, but both are bold. All letters in LIBERTY are visible. Reverse: Half of the details of the eagle's feathers are clear, although wings and legs exhibit wear spots. Motto is clear. Wear apparent on the shield, but most details are discernable.

VF-30: Light wear on design elements. Obverse: Wear spots apparent on Liberty's cheek, hair and cap as well as leaves. Bottom leaves are weak but some details are visible. Folds in Liberty's cap are complete and LIBERTY and band are complete. Reverse: Most feather details on eagle's neck and tail are clear. All details on the shield are clear, although wear evident. Motto is complete.

EF-40: Light wear present on design high points. Obverse: Light wear shows on Liberty's cheek, hair above forehead, cap and on the leaves. Word LIBERTY is sharp and edges of band are clear. Reverse: Light wear visible on high points of eagle's head, neck, wings and tail but details are clearly defined. No trace of wear on edges of leaves. Traces of Mint luster may show.

EF-45: Very light wear on design high points. Obverse: Slight wear detectable on high points of upper leaves, Liberty's cheek and hair above forehead. Edges of band are bold and LIBERTY is sharp. Reverse: Slight wear discernable on high points of eagle's head, neck, wings and talons. Centerlines of eagle's tail feathers are clearly defined. Part of Mint luster is present.

AU-50: Small traces of wear visible on design high points. Obverse: Traces of wear show on Liberty's cheek and on her hair below the LIBERTY headband. Reverse: Traces of wear show on eagle's head, neck, tips of wings and tail. Half of Mint luster present.

AU-55: Very small traces of wear on design high points. Obverse: Slight trace of wear shows on highest points of hair below BER in LIBERTY on the headband. Reverse: Trace of wear detectable on eagle's head, tips of wings and tips of tail. Three-quarters of Mint luster present.

AU-58: Slightest traces of wear detectable on design high points. Obverse: Some evidence of abrasion on high points of Liberty's cheek and her hair below LIBERTY headband. Reverse: Some signs of abrasion on eagle's head, tips of tail and tips of wings.

MS-60: Strictly Uncirculated. No traces of wear detectable on the coin. May have large detracting contact marks or damage spots or may be heavily toned. May have heavy concentrations of hairline scratches or large areas of unattractive scuff marks. May have rim nicks. Coin may appear to be dull or washed out. May lack full Mint luster. Eye appeal is generally poor.

MS-61: Strictly Uncirculated. No traces of wear detectable. Surfaces may exhibit large and small clusters of contact marks as well as noticeable hairline scratches. Scuff marks may be present on major design elements. Rim nicks and planchet defects may show. Mint luster may be diminished or noticeably impaired. Eye appeal is somewhat unattractive.

MS-62: Strictly Uncirculated. No traces of wear detectable. A few large marks or nicks are permitted in the prime focal areas. Hairline scratches may be very noticeable. Large, unattractive scuff marks may be evident on major design elements. May exhibit dull luster. Overall eye appeal is generally acceptable.

MS-63: Strictly Uncirculated. No traces of wear detectable. A few scattered heavy contact marks and numerous small contact marks may be evident. Hairline scratches are visible without magnification. Several detracting scuff marks or defects may be present on the design elements or in the fields. Mint luster may be slightly impaired. Overall, the coin is rather attractive.

MS-64: Strictly Uncirculated. No traces of wear detectable. One or two moderately heavy contact marks may be present as well as several small contact marks in groups. One or two small patches of hairline scratches permitted when seen under low magnification. Noticeable light scuff marks may be evident on design elements or in the fields. Exhibits average luster and strike. Overall, the coin is attractive and has pleasing eye appeal.

MS-65: Strictly Uncirculated. No traces of wear detectable. A few, small scattered contact marks permitted or two larger marks. One or two small patches of hairline scratches (visible under magnification) acceptable. Light scuff marks may show on design high points. Displays attractive and high quality luster and strike for the date and Mint. Overall quality is above average and eye appeal is very pleasing.

MS-66: Strictly Uncirculated. No traces of wear detectable. No more than two or three minor, but noticeable contact marks permitted. A few, very light hairline scratch marks visible under magnification are allowed. One or two light scuff marks may show on frosted surfaces of design elements or in the fields. Must exhibit above average quality of strike and full, original Mint luster. Eye appeal must be above average and very pleasing for the date and Mint.

Standing Liberty Quarter Dollar

Many say the Standing Liberty quarter dollar – one of the most beautiful U.S. coin designs – is one of the most difficult coins to grade in the U.S. series. Their opinions are supported by both the complexity of the obverse design and the fact the Standing Liberty design underwent a major modification early and a minor change later in the 14 years it was produced.

Sculptor Hermon MacNeil used the full canvas of the 24.26-millimeter 25-cent planchet for his allegorical depiction of Liberty.

The Bureau of the Mint's official discourse, published in Director Robert W. Wooley's 1916 annual report, states that the design "… is intended to typify in a measure the awakening interest of the country to its own protection."

Wooley notes that on the obverse "… Liberty is shown as a full-length figure, front view, with head turned toward the left, stepping forward to the gateway of the country, and on the wall are inscribed the words IN GOD WE TRUST. … The left arm of the figure of Liberty is upraised, bearing the shield in the attitude of protection, from which the covering is being drawn. The right hand bears the olive branch of peace. On the field above the head is inscribed the word LIBERTY, and on the step under her feet 1916."

Noting that by law a representation of the American eagle is required on the reverse, Wooley describes the eagle as being "… in full flight, with wings extended, sweeping across the coin." He also notes that 13 stars connect the inscriptions on the outer circle of the design.

Curiously, with such detailed descriptions, Wooley never mentions the one detail that would raise this design to legendary status and that would become the object of change only months after the coin entered circulation.

What the Mint director didn't say is that Liberty's right breast is bare in the design as originally issued. Midway through 1917 a modified design was released and Liberty's bare breast was covered with a coat of chain mail and the stars on the reverse were rearranged.

The Mint's official explanation was that "… the recently adopted design for the quarter dollar has been modified slightly for the purpose of increasing its artistic merit …" The law authorizing the changes stipulated that " … No changes shall be made in the emblems or devices used. The modifications shall consist of the changing of the position of the eagle, the rearrangement of the stars and lettering, and a slight concavity given to the surface."

For whatever reason, direct comparison of the original and modified designs suggests the Mint ventured beyond its authorization. The design changes are a starting point for grading.

The original design is referenced differently, depending on which source you use. Most dealers and books such as J.H. Cline's *Standing Liberty Quarters* and Professional Coin Grading Service's *Official Guide to Coin Grading and Counterfeit Detection*, refer to the original design as Type I (1). The American Numismatic Association's *Official ANA Grading Standards for U.S. Coins* uses the term Variety I. *Coin World's Coin Values* uses the descriptive term Bare Breast.

The modified design, issued beginning in mid-1917, is known as Type II (2), Variety I or Mailed Breast, Stars Below Eagle.

A few specialists refer to the strengthening of the date in 1925 and classify coins produced from 1925 through 1930 as Type III (3). Others denote the date modification as "later" Type II (2).

In the grade descriptions in this book, Type 1 and Type 2 are used in that it appears to be the most widely used style and it is the shortest descriptor.

Because of the design differences, ANA's grading guide lists separate criteria for Variety I and Variety II coins. PCGS notes there are "slight variances in grading Type I and Type II Standing Liberty quarters, but there are more similarities than differences. The head and shield detail and the lack of the three stars under the eagle are the most obvious differences between the two types, but in circulated grades this is insignificant."

Strike is a critical aspect of grading Standing Liberty quarter dollars. Specialists note that generally the 1917 Standing Liberty, Bare Breast quarter dollars exhibit the best strike of the series, but even within this issue weakness is sometimes visible on Liberty's head and shield on the obverse and on the eagle's body on the reverse as well as the leading part of his wing. Many of the 1916 and 1917 Bare Breast coins exhibit weakness on Liberty's head, breast, shield and leg on the obverse and the eagle's body and wing on the reverse.

Modifications made in 1917 did not improve the striking characteristics. Many of the Mailed Breast, Stars Below Eagle coins – especially those struck at the Denver and San Francisco Mints – show weakness in Liberty's head, breast, shield and right leg and these details are often incomplete. And on the reverse, the eagle's body and the leading edge of his right wing usually exhibit some incompleteness. Dates, especially on 1917 to 1924 quarter dollars, are often weakly struck.

The most prized (and valuable) Standing Liberty quarter dollars – regardless of date – are those that have a "full head." The same grading criteria are used regardless of whether Miss Liberty's head is completely present. Full head is designated with an "FH" following the numerical grade. In some pricing guides, only "H" is used to denote full head

The Standing Liberty Quarter Collectors Society defines "full head" for the Bare Breast (Type I or Variety I) as having "a complete definite raised line of hairline separation from the forehead, cheekbone and throat areas. The design must be continuous, even though the border line may not." To earn the full head for the Mailed Breast, Stars Below Eagle (Type II or Variety II) the SLQCS requires: "The three leaves (sprigs) must be complete down to their connecting point, the ear hole must be visible, and there must be a complete, unbroken hair line from the forehead to the jaw area and around under the ear hole to its termination at the back of the neck."

PCGS delineates different criteria for full head for 1916 Type I, 1917 Type I, 1917 to 1924 Type II and 1925 to 1930 Type II.

Full Head of the Type 1 design found on Standing Liberty quarters dated 1916 and 1917.

Type 2 Full Head found on coins from 1917 through 1930.

Not Full Head on Type 2 coins produced from 1917 through 1930.

MS-63

MS-64

MS-65

Type 1 Full Head specimens of 1917 Standing Liberty quarters are shown in three Mint State grades. The number of contact marks, hairline scratches and amount of luster account for the incremental differences. Each of these factors is difficult to discern without rotating the coin.

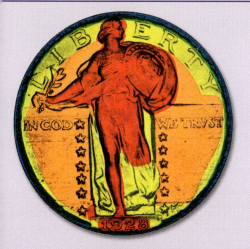

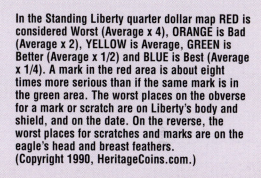

In the Standing Liberty quarter dollar map RED is considered Worst (Average x 4), ORANGE is Bad (Average x 2), YELLOW is Average, GREEN is Better (Average x 1/2) and BLUE is Best (Average x 1/4). A mark in the red area is about eight times more serious than if the same mark is in the green area. The worst places on the obverse for a mark or scratch are on Liberty's body and shield, and on the date. On the reverse, the worst places for scratches and marks are on the eagle's head and breast feathers. (Copyright 1990, HeritageCoins.com.)

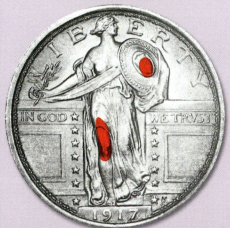

Wear is detected first on the high points of the coin's design, which are highlighted in red. On the obverse of the Standing Liberty quarter dollar, high points are on Liberty's right knee and thigh showing through her gown and on the center of the shield covering her left arm and shoulder. On the reverse, the high points are on the eagle's breast and edge of its left wing. (Copyright 1990, HeritageCoins.com.)

117

FR-2: Date faintly readable for Type 1 and 1917 to 1924 Type 2 coins. Part of date readable on later Type 2 coins. Rims on both obverse and reverse worn into lettering, stars and fields. Slight inner details visible on otherwise flat Liberty. On reverse, for both types, no feathers visible. Some lettering and stars worn away.

AG-3: Date readable but partially worn away on Type 1 and 1917 to 1924 Type 2 coins. Date more complete on later Type 2 coins. Figure is outlined with nearly all details worn away on both types. Legend weak but readable and may merge into rim on Type 1. Legend readable and half worn away on Type 2; may merge with rim. Entire design partially worn away on reverse and some letters merging into rim for both types.

G-6: For both Type 1 and Type 2, entire obverse design is well worn with little detail remaining. Legends are weak but readable. Top of date may be worn flat, but rim is complete. Date is barely readable on early Type 2. On the reverse, eagle is worn almost flat but is completely outlined. Stars and lettering worn, but clearly visible. Rim worn to tops of legends.

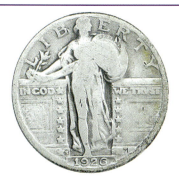

G-6: Wear on later-date Type 2 (1925 through 1930) coins is generally the same as Type 1 and Type 2 early dates (1917 through 1924) except for the date area. Almost all of date should be clear and readable.

VG-8: For both types, entire design on obverse is weak with most details on Liberty's gown worn smooth. Rim is complete. On Type 1 all letters and date are clear, drapery across breast is outlined and bottom right star is worn flat. On Type 2, all letters are clear but numerals only partially readable and drapery across breast is partially outlined. Reverse: Large feathers at ends of wings are well separated, eye is visible and rim is complete.

VG-8: Wear on later-date Type 2 (1925 through 1930) coins is generally the same as Type 1 and Type 2 early dates (1917 through 1924) except for the date area. Date should be clear.

F-12: On Type 1 obverse, gown details worn nearly smooth across Liberty's body, but show at sides. Right leg is nearly flat, toe is worn. Breast is worn but visible. Date is clear. On Type 2, gown details show clearly across body, although worn. Breast is worn, but some mail is visible. Date may show some weakness. On both types rim is full and outer edge of shield is complete. Reverse for both types: Eagle's breast is worn almost smooth. Half of wing feathers are visible, although well worn in spots; rim is full.

F-12: Wear on later-date Type 2 (1925 through 1930) coins is generally the same as Type 1 and Type 2 early dates (1917 through 1924) except for the date area. Date should be clear and very readable.

VF-30: Obverse: Both types wear spots show on Liberty's breast, shield and leg, gown line crossing thigh is partially visible. Circle around inner shield complete. On Type 1, wear also evident on Liberty's head. Right leg is rounded but worn from above knee almost to foot. On Type 2, right leg is rounded but worn from above knee to ankle. Half of mail covering breast can be seen. Reverse: On both types, eagle's feather ends and folds are visible in right wing. Date weak on early Type 2.

VF-30: Wear on later-date Type 2 (1925 through 1930) coins is generally the same as Type 1 and Type 2 early dates (1917 through 1924) except for the date area. Date should be clear and bold.

EF-40: Traces of mint luster may show. Obverse: On both types: Wear evident on Liberty's breast and right leg above and below knee. On Type 1, at least half of the gown line crossing the thigh is visible. On Type 2, most of the gown lines are visible, shield details are bold and breast is well rounded but has small flat spot. Reverse: On both types, high points of eagle are lightly worn, as is central part of edge on right wing. Traces of Mint luster may show.

EF-45: Some luster may show. Obverse: On both types, shield details bold. Type 1: Small flat spots visible on Liberty's right leg, knee. Most of gown line crossing thigh clear. Breast lightly worn but full and rounded. Type 2: Almost all of gown lines clearly visible. Breast lightly worn, may show small flat spot. Reverse: On both types, small flat spots show on high points of eagle's breast.

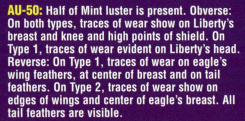

AU-50: Half of Mint luster is present. Obverse: On both types, traces of wear show on Liberty's breast and knee and high points of shield. On Type 1, traces of wear evident on Liberty's head. Reverse: On Type 1, traces of wear on eagle's wing feathers, at center of breast and on tail feathers. On Type 2, traces of wear show on edges of wings and center of eagle's breast. All tail feathers are visible.

AU-55: Three-quarters of Mint luster is present. Obverse: On Type 1 only a trace of wear evident on highest points of Liberty's head, breast, inner shield and right leg above knee. On Type 2 only a trace of wear shows on highest points of mail covering breast, inner shield and right knee. Reverse: On Type 1 a trace of wear shows on edges of wings, breast and tail feathers. On Type 2 a trace of wear evident on eagle's breast and edges of wings.

AU-58: Obverse: On Type 1 some signs of abrasion of Liberty's breast, knee and high points of shield. On Type 2 some signs of abrasion of mail covering Liberty's breast, knee, high points of gown and shield. Reverse: On both types, signs of abrasions on high points of eagle's breast and wings.

MS-61: Uncirculated with no trace of wear for both types. May have a few heavy or numerous light contact marks in prime and secondary focal areas. May have noticeable patch or continuous hairline scratches over surfaces. Luster may be original or impaired. Generally unattractive eye appeal.

MS-62: Uncirculated with no trace of wear for both types. May have distracting marks in prime or secondary focal areas. May have a few, noticeable scattered patches of hairline scratches. Luster may be original or impaired. Generally acceptable eye appeal.

MS-63: Uncirculated with no trace of wear for both types. May have distracting marks in prime focal areas and a few scattered or small hairline scratches. Luster may be original or slightly impaired. Eye appeal should be rather attractive.

MS-64: Uncirculated with no trace of wear for both types. May have light scattered marks, with a few in prime focal areas. May have a few scattered hairline scratches in secondary areas. Must have average to full original luster and pleasing eye appeal.

MS-65: Uncirculated with no trace of wear for both types. Light and scattered contact marks permitted, but not in prime focal areas. May have a few scattered hairline scratches. Luster must be fully original and eye appeal must be very pleasing.

MS-66: Uncirculated with no trace of wear for both types. Several small contact marks permitted, with a few in prime focal areas. No hairline scratches permitted unless detectable under magnification. Must have above average, fully original luster. Must have above average eye appeal.

Washington Quarter Dollar

Through the centuries, George Washington may have been first in the hearts of his countrymen. But few Americans in 1932 set aside the first U.S. circulating coin to bear his likeness.

Struck and issued to honor the bicentennial of Washington's birth in 1932, few then could have envisioned the design's longevity on the quarter dollar denomination. A modified, smaller version of John Flanagan's left-facing portrait of Washington continues the line via State quarter dollars, issued since 1999.

A left-facing, full-figure heraldic eagle dominates the reverse of the Washington quarter dollar and leaves virtually no space in the field of the coin. A Bicentennial reverse replaced the eagle for a two-year period in 1975 and 1976 and the 50 State reverses will occupy the "tails" side until the 10-year program concludes in 2008.

Our grading focus is on the Flanagan designs from 1932 through 1998 and the eagle for the same period, sans the two-year Bicentennial break.

Early Washington quarter dollars, struck from 1932 through the 1964 date, are composed of 90 percent silver and wear much more readily than the later copper-nickel clad issues, produced beginning in 1965.

Contact marks can be a problem with the early silver Washington quarter dollars, especially those from the 1930s, which exhibit marks on Washington's cheek or neck, or the fields in front of his face. However, collector abuse is also a factor in the early Washington quarter dollars. Many have been cleaned, scratched or subjected to some form of abuse. Luster quality on these abused coins is well below average.

PVC (polyvinyl chloride) contamination (leaching from holders containing the plasticizer) is another problem that has greatly affected Washington quarter dollars over the years.

Most flips used by auction houses in the 1990s contained PVC. Despite the fact that the auction firms warned their customers not to store coins long term in the auction flips, time has shown that many left their coins in them too long. By the time they submitted the Washington quarter dollars for professional grading, many showed obvious signs of white, hazy or bright green surface PVC contamination. Major grading services will not grade such coins until the contamination is removed.

Another common problem is the storage of Washington quarter dollars in old, crispy flips with multiple staple holes. Many early Washington quarter dollars exhibit signs of hairline scratches that in all likelihood were caused by the staple holes coming into contact with the surfaces of the coins.

To avoid additional problems, prudent collectors today would do well to use fresh polybags, fresh flips and flips that are free of PVC contaminants to house their coins.

Hairline scratches are a significant problem with this issue. Often, the hairlines are seen on the cheek, neck or the fields in front of the face. Examine Washington quarter dollars carefully with a top-quality magnifier. Tilt them side to side and up and down as you check for scratches or evidence of cleaning.

Altered dates and counterfeiting are particular challenging problems for the first decade of Washington quarter dollars. Thousands of bogus 1932-D and 1932-S Washington quarter dollars have been identified by the professional grading services. They were created by adding spurious D or S Mint marks to genuine 1932 coins struck at the Philadelphia Mint without a Mint mark. Additionally, the technique of adding a Mint mark to a genuine coin has produced significant quantities of fake 1934-D, 1935-D, 1936-D, 1937-S, 1938-S, 1939-S and 1940-D Washington quarter dollars. In the 1980s, rolls of counterfeit Brilliant Uncirculated 1934 Washington quarter dollars surfaced. They were die-struck counterfeits that featured extra-sharp reeding (as seen on Proof quarters) and unnatural Mint luster.

Strike can play a role in grading Washington quarter dollars. Some early dates, especially those struck at Branch Mints, tend to be weakly struck and lack design details, even on Uncirculated examples. Thus, one must learn to distinguish between weak striking and legitimate wear.

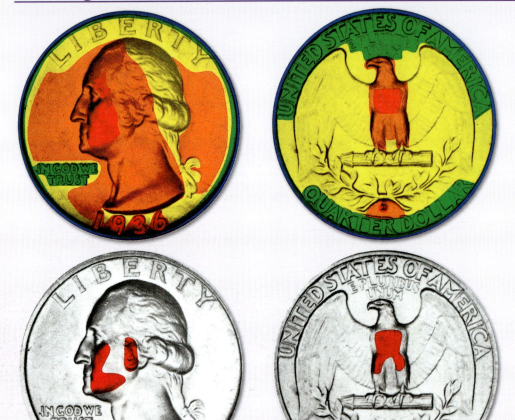

In the Washington quarter dollar map RED is considered Worst (Average x 4), ORANGE is Bad (Average x 2), YELLOW is Average, GREEN is Better (Average x 1/2) and BLUE is Best (Average x 1/4). A mark in the red area is about eight times more serious than if the same mark is in the green area. The worst places on the obverse for a mark or scratch are on Washington's temple, cheek and jaw, and the date. On the reverse, the worst places for scratches and marks are on the eagle's breast feathers.
(Copyright 1990, HeritageCoins.com.)

Wear is detected first on the high points of the coin's design, which are highlighted in red. On the obverse of the Washington quarter dollar high points are on the front part of his cheek and jaw and the curls of hair in front of the ear. Highest points on the reverse are the eagle's breast feathers and upper thighs.
(Copyright 1990, HeritageCoins.com.)

AG-3: Parts of legend and date are worn smooth. Obverse: Washington's head is outlined, but nearly all details are worn away. The date is readable, but worn. Traces of the motto are visible and the legend appears to be merging into the rim. Reverse: Entire design partially worn away, with rim merging into legend.

VG-8: Design elements well worn, but clear and flat. Lacks details. Obverse: All details on the head weak, with most of the details in the hair worn smooth. Reverse: Approximately half of the eagle's wing feathers are visible. Eagle's breast and legs outlined. Leaves below perch show very little detail. The rim is complete.

F-12: The entire design is clear and bold although there is considerable even wear. Obverse: Hair details show only at back of head. Motto is clearly visible, but weak. Part of the edge of Washington's cheek is worn away. Reverse: Eagle's breast and leg feathers are worn smooth. Parts of wings are nearly smooth. Some detail visible in leaves.

F-15: Even wear, although entire design is clear and bold. Obverse: About half of the details discernable on Washington's hair. Reverse: Some details in eagle's breast and leg feathers evident. Legends are bolder, although worn.

VF-20: Light to moderate wear. Obverse: Three-fourths of hair details show on Washington's head. Some hair details around his ear are visible. His cheek is bold but lightly worn. Reverse: Wear shows on eagle's breast, but a few feathers are detectable. Eagle's lower legs are worn smooth. Most details in eagle's wings are clear.

VF-30: All major design features are sharp. Obverse: Hair lines are weak, but display nearly full details. Spots of wear evident on hair at forehead and ear. Wear spots also observable on cheek and jaw. Reverse: Wear shows on eagle's breast, but some feather details present. Feathers on legs are worn smooth. All vertical wing feathers are clear.

EF-40: Wear present on most of the design high points. Obverse: Wear visible on high points of Washington's hair around his ear and hairline up to his crown. Reverse: Light wear on high points of eagle's breast, legs and claws. However, all details are clearly defined and are partially separated. Some Mint luster is present.

EF-45: Light wear on highest points of designs. Obverse: Slight wear detectable on high points of hair around ear and along Washington's hairline up to his crown. Lines in hair are sharp and detailed. Reverse: Wear shows on high points of eagle's legs. Breast feathers are worn but clearly defined and fully separated. Half of Mint luster present.

AU-50: Traces of wear visible on design high points. Obverse: Traces of wear evident on hair in front of and in back of Washington's ear. Reverse: Trace of wear shows on the eagle's breast feathers and legs. Three-fourths of Mint luster remains.

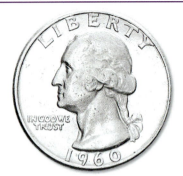

AU-55: Small traces of wear detectable on highest points of design devices. Obverse: Slight trace of wear shows on highest points of hair curls in front and in back of ear. Reverse: A slight trace of wear evident on highest points of eagle's breast feathers. Nearly all of the Mint luster remains.

AU-58: Barest traces of wear evident on one or more of the design's high points. Obverse: Some signs of abrasion may be seen on high point of Washington's cheek and hair in front and back of ear. Reverse: Barest trace of wear detectable on eagle's breast feathers and tops of legs. Nearly full Mint luster present and no detracting contact marks. Coin exhibits attractive eye appeal.

MS-60: Uncirculated. No trace of wear on design high points. Unattractive, dull or washed out Mint luster often encountered. May have many large detracting contact marks or damage spots. May have noticeable patches of or continuous hairlines scratches throughout. Generally poor eye appeal.

MS-61: Uncirculated. No trace of wear on design high points. Diminished Mint luster throughout as well as clusters of large and small contact marks. Small rim nicks, striking or planchet defects may show. Eye appeal is generally unattractive.

MS-62: Uncirculated. No trace of wear on design high points. Mint luster may be dull or impaired. Clusters of small marks may be present overall with a few large nicks or marks in the prime focal areas. Hairline scratches may be very noticeable. Strike, rim and planchet quality may be noticeably average. Eye appeal overall is generally acceptable.

MS-63: Uncirculated. No trace of wear on design high points. Exhibits attractive Mint luster but may contain distracting contact marks in prime focal areas. May have a few scattered or small patches of hairline scratches. Overall, has attractive eye appeal.

131

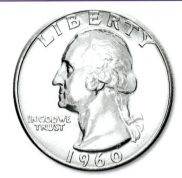

MS-64: Uncirculated. No trace of wear on design high points. May have light, scattered contact marks, with a few in prime focal areas. May have a few scattered or small hairline scratches in secondary areas. Mint luster should be at least average. Exhibits pleasing eye appeal.

MS-65: Uncirculated. No trace of wear on design high points. Nearly perfect. Exhibits high quality of luster and strike for the date and Mint. May have a few scattered contact marks or two larger marks. One or two small patches of hairline scratches may show under magnification. Overall eye appeal is very pleasing.

State Quarter Dollar

Currently more that 140 million Americans are collecting the State quarter dollars. The coins are struck for general circulation, but they are also offered in a multitude of collector products in different finishes in both the copper-nickel clad alloy and 90 percent silver.

The U.S. Mint produces five new reverse designs each year in 10-week intervals. Launched in 1999, the program is scheduled to conclude in 2008.

A modified version of John Flanagan's portrait of George Washington serves as the common obverse. Each reverse design has a different theme. They are selected by the state being honored, but all are rendered by U.S. Mint sculptor-engravers from design concepts or word descriptions.

The State copper-nickel clad quarter dollars are struck in very low relief, which adds to circulation longevity. Most important for many who are collecting from pocket change, it is highly possible to find State quarter dollars in circulation that do not exhibit any traces of wear on the design high points, the places to first spot wear. (Design high points for each State quarter dollar are highlighted in red on the following pages.) Any wear on the design high points relegates the coin to circulated.

If no evidence of wear is on the design high points, a State quarter dollar can be deemed Uncirculated. However, the number of contact marks and scratches will determine its score on the 11-point Mint State scale.

Contact marks in prime focal areas are the biggest problem for State quarter dollars. Most have too many contact marks to be rated in the higher Mint State range. Contact marks are attained after the design is stamped onto the coin planchet in the coining chamber. The coins drop from the coining presses into large tubs and strike other coins. In some cases, the coins drop into bags. In either case, the coins clang against each other, giving and receiving nicks and scratches.

The coins of the first three years of issue – 1999, 2000 and 2001 – tend to have greater numbers of contact marks on the Uncirculated coins. Fewer contact marks (better quality) beginning in 2003 has been attributed to the fact that the Mint is bagging fewer of the quarter dollars and instead ships most of its coins in tubs to firms such as Brinks, which roll and box the quarters for distribution to banks. The latest process moves the individual coins around less, creating a higher probability of fewer contact marks.

Professional graders observe that most of the State quarter dollars sorted from rolls and bags average in the Mint State 64 and MS-65 range.

A review of reports published by the three major grading services that regularly make public the numbers of coins they have graded – Professional Coin Grading Service, Numismatic Guaranty Corporation of America and ANACS – shows MS-66 to be the most common grade for the State copper-nickel clad quarter dollars that have been submitted for grading. An estimated 80 percent or more of the State quarter dollars garnering the lofty MS-66 and higher grades are being taken from Uncirculated Mint sets rather than from rolls and bags. The coins in later Mint sets are struck on slower-speed presses at higher pressures than used for making circulating examples. The Uncirculated Mint set coins receive more care at the Mint and are packaged separately from the coins that are shipped in bulk.

Professional graders note that few circulation strikes meet the requirements for grades above MS-66. They contrast that with significant numbers of high-grade Proof copper-nickel clad and silver versions of the State quarter dollars, the majority of which are commanding Proof 68 and Proof 69 grades.

Eye appeal or the overall attractiveness is the most important component of grading Uncirculated clad State quarter dollars. Contact marks in the field areas (where no design elements are present) or in prominent areas of the design, for example on Washington's cheek on the obverse, are the most detrimental. A simple rule of thumb is useful to remember: A large number of small contact marks won't lower the grade as much as one or two large contact marks in prominent, noticeable areas of the field and design elements.

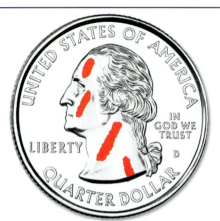

Delaware: Caesar Rodney's left arm from shoulder to elbow, horse's left shoulder and thigh.

Pennsylvania: Left, top portion of Commonwealth's dress and dress covering left leg from thigh to bottom of dress.

New Jersey: Washington's left upper arm and cape, shoulder of soldier with oar at rear, right arm of soldier with oar in middle of boat, floating ice chunk.

Georgia: Across left half of w in WISDOM ribbon on left and center of the peach.

Connecticut: Main trunk of the Charter Oak.

Massachusetts: Minuteman's right arm from elbow to hand holding gun, front thighs and base below left foot.

135

Maryland: Top dome of the historic Maryland Statehouse and roof line, front rib of larger dome and three windows below the large dome.

South Carolina: Feathers on the head, back and upper wing of South Carolina wren, trunk of palmetto tree.

New Hampshire: Center of head, eyebrow, temple, left side of nose and cheekbone and lower neck of Old Man of the Mountain formation.

Virginia: Centers of the skysail and mainsail, forward mast sail and hull of the *Susan Constant*, and both sails of the *Discovery*.

New York: Upper northeast and central eastern sectors of New York state, central front portions of Statue of Liberty's garb.

North Carolina: Center top of Wright Flyer, lower back portion of Wilbur Wright's jacket and full length of right trouser leg, bench in sand in foreground.

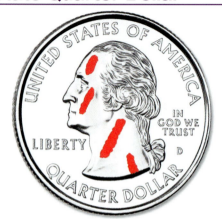

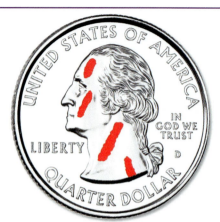

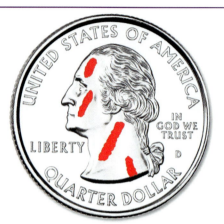

Rhode Island: Upper and lower right side of mainsail and lower center of jib sail.

Vermont: Trunks of both maple trees and center back of man's jacket.

Kentucky: Upper left corner of Federal Hill beneath roof line, three fence posts, and horse's jaw, mane and croup.

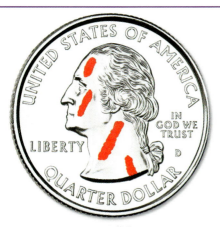

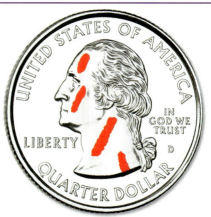

Tennessee: Guitar fretboard, neck and strings of fiddle, trumpet bell, and top, center corners of music book.

Ohio: Top of astronaut's helmet faceplate, center of chest, middle of astronaut's right side and left thigh.

Louisiana: Trumpet bell, head and wing of pelican.

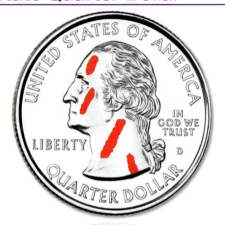

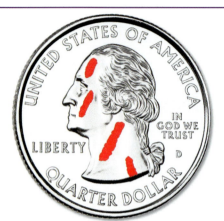

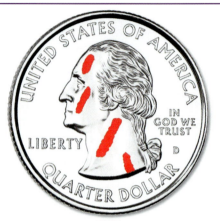

Indiana: Hood and both front tires of Indy race car.

Mississippi: Edges of magnolia blossoms and leaves.

Illinois: Chest and thighs of Abe Lincoln and lower portion of book in his right hand.

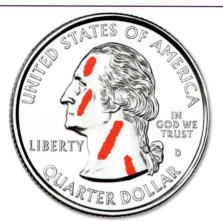

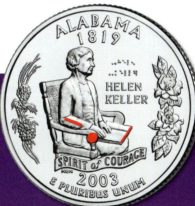

Alabama: Helen Keller's right forearm, curl in armchair rest, and top edge of Braille book.

Maine: Center portion of lighthouse, portions of embankment, first mast sail on the *Victory Chimes*.

Missouri: Upper body of middle man in boat, front left edge of boat, and parts of shoreline on both sides of the Missouri River.

Arkansas: Girdle and upper girdle facets of diamond, body of mallard duck, rice stalks and river shoreline.

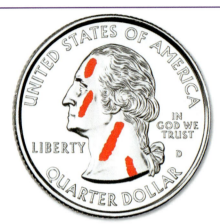

Michigan: Eastern half of the Upper Peninsula and across center forefingers and base of the thumb of the "mitten" of the Lower Peninsula.

Florida: Center of mainsail, jib sail and starboard bow of Spanish galleon; left wing and rear of space shuttle; and grass at base of two sabal palm trees.

Texas: Center edges of each section of the three-dimensional five-pointed Lone Star.

Iowa: Center of schoolhouse roof, banister and edge of right entrance steps; body of adult female holding onto tree; and distant prairie hilltop behind schoolhouse.

Wisconsin: Above cow's right eye and on cow's right nostril, center of cowbell; left and right side of removed wedge of cheese wheel; right lower portion of corn husk and lower edge of right corn leaf.

California: Right rim of John Muir's hat, upper right jacket sleeve, right shoe. Ground behind Muir's left heel, breast of condor in flight, section near top of mountain and rocks at the base.

Minnesota: Loon's eye, head and body behind neck; bow and stern of motorboat; top of outboard motor.

Oregon: Top of Wizard Island and cliffs along the north caldera wall of Crater Lake.

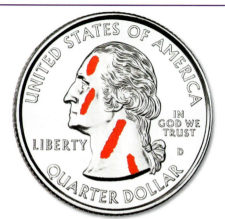

Kansas: Center of left forward sunflower; bison's lower legs, top of back, center of head, above right eye, right nostril and center of right side.

West Virginia: River bank on lower left under trees, rocks along banks of New River on lower right, just below mountain peak in center.

Barber Half Dollar

Charles E. Barber was ahead of his time. Defying high-relief advocates, he rendered his designs for circulating coins in low relief. The half dollars, quarter dollars and dimes bearing his Liberty Head design testify to the genius of the Mint's chief engraver. More than 100 years after being issued, Barber's widely circulated, low relief creations survive with many of their design elements remaining.

Most specialists and devotees of the series consider the 90 percent silver Barber half dollar easy to grade, primarily because it is a large coin (diameter 30.61 millimeters or 1.21 inches) and all of the design elements are easily viewed without the necessity of magnification.

However, David Lawrence Feigenbaum, writing under the name David Lawrence in *The Complete Guide to Barber Halves,* cautions, "Like many U.S. coins, the strike must be taken into consideration." He especially points to Barber half dollars struck at the New Orleans Mint as often being weakly struck and lacking details on Liberty's forehead, the wreath she wears in her hair, and sometimes on the LIBERTY legend on her headband. On the reverse of New Orleans Mint coins, he suggests looking for weakness of strike "along a vertical path from the right corner of the shield down to the eagle's claw."

He also explains: "Coins wear continuously, not in discrete steps, and the different standard grades represent levels in the process." Some collectors use "split grades" – assigning different grades to the obverse and reverse of a coin – although most professional third-party grading services today assign only one grade for a coin.

Grading entails assessing the condition of the surfaces on both sides of the coin. The right-facing portrait of Liberty dominates the obverse. The portrait occupies most of the obverse's surface, but there are small field areas in front of her face and behind her head. A left-facing, heraldic eagle dominates the reverse and leaves little space in the fields to either side. Thirteen five-pointed stars fill the field above the eagle's head.

Contact marks, evidence of where the coin has collided with other coins or other objects, are most often found on the large design devices – Liberty's face (especially her cheek) and neck and the date on the obverse. On the reverse, the eagle's neck and head and shield are among the most critical areas for contact marks.

In analyzing the state of the surfaces of a Barber half dollar, one must weigh the visual impact of any imperfections and weigh the degree of severity and whether the locations of the imperfections seriously detract from the coin's overall appearance.

Contact marks are permitted in the Uncirculated grades, but their number and location help to determine where the grade will ultimately land on the Mint State scale. The more contact marks, the lower the grade, especially if they detract from the overall eye appeal.

One of the most important grading decisions is determining whether there is evidence of wear on the coin's surface. That means you must be able to distinguish between a Mint State coin and a top grade About Uncirculated coin. Critical to determining whether a coin is Uncirculated is inspecting the surfaces to find evidence of wear. Graders look first at the high points of the design, where wear from circulation is most likely to appear. The design high points should be the first areas of the coin inspected. Tilt and rotate the coin, looking for a contrast of luster between the high points and the rest of the coin. Abrasions on the high points drop the grade to circulated.

Eye appeal or the aesthetic state of the coin is another important factor in grading, While it is the most subjective factor, it cannot be overlooked or discounted. Ultimately one has to take all of the coin's qualities into consideration and rank and balance them.

Professional graders suggest their best advice in grading Barber half dollars is "to grade the entire coin," rather than focusing almost exclusively on the obverse.

In the Barber half dollar map RED is considered Worst (Average x 4), ORANGE is Bad (Average x 2), YELLOW is Average, GREEN is Better (Average x 1/2) and BLUE is Best (Average x 1/4). A mark in the red area is about eight times more serious than if the same mark is in the green area. The worst places on the obverse for a mark or scratch are on Liberty's face, which is the focal point of the coin. On the reverse, the eagle's head and neck are the worst places for scratches and marks.
(Copyright 1990, HeritageCoins.com.)

Design high points on the Barber half dollar are highlighted in red. The highest points on the obverse are on Liberty's cheek and the hair just above her forehead. The highest points on the reverse are the eagle's head and neck feathers, tips of both wings and the center tail feathers.
(Copyright 1990, HeritageCoins.com.)

AG-3/FR-2: The obverse grades AG-3. Liberty's head is outlined but nearly all other details of the obverse design are worn away. The date is worn but readable and the legend is merging into the rim. The reverse grades Fair 2 because the entire rim is worn away and design details are recognizable but heavily worn.

G-6: Overall the design elements are heavily worn but the rim is complete on both sides. Obverse: Liberty is worn flat; recessed areas may show some detail. The date is readable. The rim may be worn into tops of a few letters. First letter of LIBERTY in Liberty's head wreath is identifiable. Reverse: The rim is complete except for dates and Mints known to exhibit weak strikes.

VG-8: Design elements are clear, but flat and lacking details: Obverse: Details of Liberty's face are heavily worn and entire head of Liberty area is weak. Three letters in LIBERTY are discernable. The rim is complete. Reverse: Small amounts of detail on the eagle remain. Parts of the motto and the eagle's eye are visible. Arrows and leaves are flat and most of the shield is very weak.

VG-10: More details begin to show in the design elements. Obverse: Parts of top leaves in Liberty's head wreath are visible. Five of the letters in LIBERTY are detectable. Reverse: More details begin to emerge on the eagle's wings and leg feathers and on the shield.

F-12: Considerable wear is evident. Obverse: All letters in LIBERTY are present although BER may be weak. Details are emerging on the upper row of wreath's leaves but lower row's leaves are worn smooth. Reverse: Half of eagle's feathers are visible. Horizontal shield lines are merged while the vertical lines are separated. Letters in the legend letters are worn but clear. Wear spots show in the center of the neck, motto and arrows.

F-15: Moderate wear is evident. Obverse: All letters in LIBERTY are complete, although lower part of BER may appear slightly weak. Details on the wreath evidence moderate wear but are complete. Reverse: Horizontal shield lines are separated and more details on eagle's feathers are emerging.

VF-20: Moderate even wear is visible, but all design elements are sharp. Obverse: LIBERTY is complete and Liberty's hair and ribbon are worn but bold. Half of details show in wreath's leaves. Bottom folds in Liberty's cap are full. Reverse: Half of the details of eagle's feathers are clear. Wear spots are evident on the eagle's wings, tail and legs. All shield details are worn but clear. The motto is clear.

VF-25: Obverse: Wreath on Liberty's head appears more three-dimensional although weakness is sometimes detectable near Liberty's eye. Bottom folds of Liberty's cap are fuller. Hair ribbon is more distinct. Reverse: More details are emerging on the shield and the eagle's feathers, tips of his wings and tail feathers.

VF-30: Light, even wear is evident throughout. The word LIBERTY and the headband are complete. The bottom row of leaves is weak but details are emerging. Cap folds are distinct. Reverse: All details of the shield are visible, although wear is present. Most details on the eagle's neck and tail are clear. The motto is complete on the ribbon held by the eagle's beak.

VF-35: Obverse: The word LIBERTY and Liberty's headband are complete and bold. More details are evident on the bottom row of leaves in the wreath. Ribbon details are bolder. Reverse: More feather details are emerging on eagle's neck, wing feathers and wing tips. Eagle's tail feather details are more distinct. The motto is bolder.

EF-40: Light wear is apparent on the design high points. Obverse: The word LIBERTY is sharp and the band edges are clear. Light wear is visible on leaves of the wreath and on Liberty's cheek, hair above her forehead and her cap. Reverse: Light wear can be seen on the eagle's head, neck, wings and tail, but the details are clearly defined. Traces of Mint luster are present.

EF-45: Very light wear is detectable on the design high points. Obverse: The word LIBERTY is sharp and the band edges are bold. Slight wear is detectable on high points of the upper leaves of the wreath, on Liberty's cheek and on the hair above her forehead. Reverse: High points of eagle's head, neck, wings and talons are slightly worn. The lines of the eagle's center tail feather are clearly defined. Part of the Mint luster is present.

AU-50: A trace of wear is visible on the design high points: Obverse: Liberty's cheek may be slightly flat. Traces of wear are evident on Liberty's cheek, her hair below LIBERTY in the headband and on tips of the leaves in the wreath. Reverse: Traces of wear show on the eagle's head, neck, tips of his wings and tail feathers. Half of the Mint luster is present.

AU-55: Small traces of wear are detectable on design high points. Obverse: Small trace of wear is visible on the highest points of Liberty's hair below BER in LIBERTY in the headband. Reverse: A small trace of wear can be detected on the eagle's head, tips of his wings and the tip of his tail. Three-fourths of the Mint luster is present.

AU-58: Slight trace of wear is visible on high points of the design elements. Obverse: Some signs of abrasion evident on Liberty's cheek and her hair below LIBERTY in the headband. Reverse: Some signs of abrasion are evident on eagle's head, tips of his wings and the tip of his tail. Often an AU-58 coin that would rate in the mid-Mint State range except for the slightest wear on the design high points. Nearly full Mint luster may be present.

MS-60: Strictly Uncirculated. No traces of wear detectable on the coin. May have large detracting contact marks or damage spots or may be heavily toned. May have heavy concentrations of hairline scratches or large areas of unattractive scuff marks. May have rim nicks. Coin may appear to be dull or washed out. May lack full Mint luster. Eye appeal is generally poor.

MS-62: Strictly Uncirculated. No traces of wear detectable. A few large marks or nicks are permitted in the prime focal areas. Hairline scratches may be very noticeable. Large, unattractive scuff marks may be evident on major design elements. May exhibit dull luster. Overall eye appeal is generally acceptable.

MS-63: Strictly Uncirculated. No traces of wear detectable. A few scattered heavy contact marks and numerous small contact marks may be evident. Hairline scratches are visible without magnification. Several detracting scuff marks or defects may be present on the design elements or in the fields. Mint luster may be slightly impaired. Overall, the coin is rather attractive.

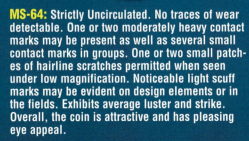

MS-64: Strictly Uncirculated. No traces of wear detectable. One or two moderately heavy contact marks may be present as well as several small contact marks in groups. One or two small patches of hairline scratches permitted when seen under low magnification. Noticeable light scuff marks may be evident on design elements or in the fields. Exhibits average luster and strike. Overall, the coin is attractive and has pleasing eye appeal.

MS-65: Strictly Uncirculated. No traces of wear detectable. A few, small scattered contact marks permitted or two larger marks. One or two small patches of hairline scratches (visible under magnification) are acceptable. Light scuff marks may show on design high points. Displays attractive and high quality luster and strike for the date and Mint. Overall quality is above average and eye appeal is very pleasing.

MS-66: Strictly Uncirculated. No traces of wear detectable. No more than two or three minor, but noticeable contact marks permitted. A few, very light hairline scratch marks visible under magnification are allowed. One or two light scuff marks may show on frosted surfaces of design elements or in the fields. Must exhibit above average quality of strike and full, original Mint luster. Eye appeal must be above average and very pleasing for the date and Mint.

Walking Liberty Half Dollar

Details. Details. Details.

The path one must follow and master to successfully grade Walking Liberty half dollars is laden with details, any one of which – if missed – could be costly. The good news is that in comparison to many other series, the Walking Liberty half dollar is considered "not that difficult" to grade.

With a diameter of 30.61 millimeters (1.21 inches), the half dollar presents a large enough canvas to capture the bold and intricate design elements.

Because the design is chock-full of details, we suggest that before embarking on your grading journey it would be helpful to study enlarged images of both the obverse and reverse of a high-grade, fully struck Walking Liberty half dollar. Such study will help to fix in your mind's eye what the coin is supposed to be. (Tip: Keep the images handy to refresh your memory, from time to time.)

Although Adolph A. Weinman's design has been hailed as one of the greatest of all time, the U.S. Mint encountered problems from the beginning in bringing out all details in a full strike. Attempts to modify the obverse were undertaken in 1918, 1937 and 1938. However, they were not entirely successful.

Thus, it should not be surprising that strike is a key characteristic and must be kept on mind when grading Walking Liberty half dollars.

The primary areas to check on the obverse are Liberty's head, left hand and the lines in her skirt.

In *The Complete Guide to Walking Liberty Half Dollars,* Bruce Fox relates that in order for a Walking Liberty half dollar to qualify as having a "full head," the "hair area between Liberty's face and bonnet must be rounded and not flat." Also, he notes that there must be separation or definition in Liberty's forehead and cheek areas, her ear, her hair below the bonnet, and above her eye and below her ear.

When inspecting Liberty's left hand at her side for evidence of a full strike, Fox specifies that the hand "must be rounded and the thumb and finger split into an obvious 'V.'" He observes that branches of laurel and oak Liberty is holding should be split at the end of the thumb as well as between the thumb and forefinger. Also, on a full strike the separation of the upper finger can be seen near the knuckles.

Fox advises that lines in Liberty's skirt are generally weak for coins struck from 1916 through 1921 and should be ignored for grading purposes. He notes that the lines in the skirt directly above the foot are generally visible in the early issues. Full strike designation on Walking Liberty half dollars constitutes visible skirt lines near the foot and also slightly above the knee.

On the reverse there is one critical area of the eagle's breast that cannot be flat or missing feathers and still merit a full-strike designation. Both Fox and Anthony Swiatek in *The Walking Liberty Half Dollar* cite specialist James Bennet Pryor's method for pinpointing the location: Draw an imaginary line from the left side of the E in the STATES legend at the top of the coin to the second L in DOLLAR of the bottom legend. Next, draw another line from the second S in STATES to the H in HALF of the bottom legend. The area below the intersection of the two imaginary lines is the location on the eagle's breast that should be closely inspected for strike.

Luster is created on the coin's surface from the microscopic flow lines as the metal flows to fill the die in the striking process. The brilliance of the luster on the surface is created by the way the metal reflects light. Specialist note that surfaces on the first two years (1916 and 1917) of the Walking Liberty half dollars exhibit a grainy, matte-like finish. Later years exhibit more luster, hence a brighter shine.

In the Walking Liberty half dollar map RED is considered Worst (Average x 4), ORANGE is Bad (Average x 2), YELLOW is Average, GREEN is Better (Average x 1/2) and BLUE is Best (Average x 1/4). A mark in the red area is about eight times more serious than if the same mark is in the green area. The worst places on the obverse for a mark or scratch are on Liberty's head, the full length of her body to the hem of the skirt covering her left leg, and the date. On the reverse, the worst places for scratches and marks are on the eagle's head and breast feathers. (Copyright 1990, HeritageCoins.com.)

High points of the design are the best places to detect wear. Peace dollar obverse high points are on Liberty's cheek and on the center portion of the bottom of her neck. On the reverse, the design high points are on the center of the eagle's wing.

Skirt lines of well-struck Walking Liberty half dollar.

Well-struck example of Liberty's head on the "Walker."

Well-struck example of Liberty's left hand on the Walking Liberty half dollar.

Well-struck example of eagle on reverse of the Walking Liberty half dollar.

AG 3: Obverse: Walking Liberty's figure is outlined and nearly all details are worn away. The legend is visible but half worn away; date is weak but readable. The rim merges with the lettering in the legend. Reverse: Eagle is outlined but all of the feather detail is worn away. Letters of the legend merge with the rim.

G-4: Obverse: Entire design is worn, with very few details remaining. The legend is readable. The date is weak but visible, although the top may be worn flat. The rim is nearly complete but flat. Reverse: Eagle is completely outlined but is worn nearly flat. Legend and motto lettering worn but clearly visible.

G-6: Obverse: All design details worn. Rim has an edge in several locations. Date and motto are virtually complete and are stronger than the G-4. Reverse: A few feathers are detectable on the eagle's upper and lower left wing. Edge of rim visible in several locations.

VG-8: Obverse: Entire design is weak and well worn, but is clear. Drapery across Liberty's body is partially visible, but most details on skirt are worn smooth. Half of the lines on the skirt must show for coins struck after 1921. All letters in legends and date are clear. Top of the motto may be weak. Rim is complete. Reverse: A third of eagle's feathers are visible. Large feathers on ends of wings are well separated. Eagle's eye is visible. All letters are clear and rim is full.

VG-10: Obverse: Outline of Liberty's right breast begins to emerge. Laurel and oak branches carried in Liberty's left hand are bolder than in VG-8. Reverse: A third of eagle's large feathers and two-thirds of small feathers on eagle's left wing are visible.

F-12: Obverse: Lines in Liberty's skirt are clear, except on coins struck before 1921, where only half are visible. Right leg is worn slightly. Liberty's left leg is worn nearly flat and sandal is worn but visible. Center of Liberty's torso is worn, but some of her garment is visible. Reverse: Eagle's breast is worn smooth. Half of wing feathers are visible although well worn in spots. Rim is full. Top two layers of feathers can be seen on left wing.

F-15: Obverse: Liberty's right breast is almost completely outlined and her left breast is beginning to show. More details on the sandal can be seen. Liberty's body appears to be more rounded and looks more sculptured. Reverse: Two-thirds of eagle's feathers are visible and the eagle's body appears to be more rounded.

VF-20: Obverse: Liberty's left breast is full, but outline is weak. Her body is somewhat rounded, especially left leg down to her knee. Wear spots show on her head, breast, arms and foot. Lines on her skirts are visible, but may be weak on coins struck before 1921. Reverse: Entire eagle is lightly worn but most major details are visible. Eagle's breast, central part of legs and top edge of right wing are worn flat.

VF-30: Obverse: All major features are sharp although wear shows on head, breasts, arms and legs. Left leg is rounded but worn from above knee to ankle. Gown line crossing Liberty's body is partially visible. Knee is flat. Liberty's left breast outline is complete and both breasts begin to appear three-dimensional. Reverse: Pupil in eagle's eye is visible. Eagle's breast and legs are clearly separated but are moderately worn and some feathers are visible between them. Feather ends and folds are distinct on right wing.

VF-35: Obverse: Wear spots evident on Liberty's head, breasts, arms and legs. Most of lines in her skirt are visible and more folds in garment draping shoulders are visible. Details of sandal are clearer. Lines in Liberty's gown clearer than in VF-30. Reverse: Greater overall definition of feathers on eagle's wings and breast. Full detail of eagle's beak present.

EF-40: Obverse: Wear shows on Liberty's head, breasts, arms and left leg. Nearly all lines on Liberty's garment are present. Details on sandal are complete. Flatness apparent on Liberty's knee. Breasts appear to be more raised and rounded than on lower grades. Reverse: All of eagle's wing feathers are distinct and bold. High points on eagle are slightly worn. Half of breast and leg feathers are visible. Central feathers below eagle's neck are well worn. Traces of Mint luster present.

EF-45: Obverse: Light wear spots evident on Liberty's head, breasts, arms, left leg and foot. Virtually all lines in gown are clear. Sandal details are bold and complete. Knee is lightly worn but full and rounded. Reverse: Small flat spots show on high points of eagle's breast and legs. Nearly full detail present on wing feathers. Part of Mint luster remains.

AU-50: Obverse: Traces of wear visible on Liberty's head, breasts, arms and left leg. Half of Mint luster is still present. Reverse: Traces of wear show on the high points of the eagle's wings and the center of his head and breast. Leg feathers are complete.

AU-53: Obverse: Slight traces of wear can be seen on Liberty's head, breasts, arms and left leg. Definition of Liberty's garment stronger overall. Slightly more Mint luster evident than on AU-50. Reverse: Slight traces of wear on high points of eagle's wings, head, and breast. Eagle's body appears rounder and fuller than on AU-50.

AU-55: Obverse: Only a trace of wear shows on highest points of Liberty's head, breasts and right arm. Reverse: A trace of wear is visible on the eagle's left leg between the breast and left wing. Three-quarters of the original Mint luster is still present.

AU-58: Small trace of wear visible on highest design points. Obverse: Signs of abrasion detectable on Liberty's hair above temple, right arm, left breast. Reverse: May detect slight abrasion on highest points of eagle's head, breast, legs and wings.

MS-60: Uncirculated coin with no traces of wear. May lack full Mint luster and surfaces may be dull, spotted or heavily toned. A few small spots may be weakly struck. May have heavy contact marks in all areas and noticeable partial or continuous hairline scratches throughout. Eye appeal is often poor.

MS-61: Uncirculated coin with no traces of wear. May have a few heavy or many light contact marks in prime and secondary focal areas. May contain noticeable patches or continuous hairline scratches on surfaces of the coin. Luster may be original or impaired. Eye appeal is generally unattractive.

MS-62: Uncirculated coin with no traces of wear. May have distracting contact marks in prime and secondary focal areas. May have a few scattered or small patches of hairline scratches. May exhibit original or impaired luster. Eye appeal is generally acceptable.

MS-63: Mint State coin with attractive, original Mint luster. May contain distracting contact marks in prime focal areas and a few scattered hairline scratches. Overall appearance is attractive.

MS-64: Attractive Mint State coin containing average to full Mint luster. May have light, scattered contact marks – a few in the prime focal areas. May have a few small, scattered hairline scratches. Overall eye appeal is pleasing.

MS-65: Mint State coin with no trace of wear. It is a nearly perfect coin except for a few small blemishes or minute nicks and contact marks. Contains full, original Mint luster. May be unevenly toned or lightly finger-marked. Overall eye appeal is very pleasing.

Franklin Half Dollar

The Franklin half dollar, with a diameter of 30.61 millimeters or 1.21 inches, in relative terms ranks in the class of larger U.S. coins. Yet, its size does not render it easy to grade.

The Franklin half dollar was struck from 1948 through 1963. Benjamin Franklin's portrait is depicted on the obverse and a representation of the Liberty Bell is the dominant design element on the reverse. To satisfy the legal mandate of an eagle being on the reverse, a small eagle stands to the right of the bell.

Grading difficulty stems from many 1950s coins that look softly struck, which feature less than bold details for a high-relief design. Especially for beginners, who have not had the opportunity to examine hundreds of Franklin half dollars for each year of issue and from each Mint or production facility, the challenge can be formidable.

Strike is not the only potential problem graders face when examining Franklin half dollars. Rick Tomaska, author of *The Complete Guide to Franklin Half Dollars,* warns that all fully struck Franklins do not look alike. "Some have far more sharply defined detail on the bust of Franklin on the obverse and on the Liberty Bell on the reverse than others." This characteristic is due to wear of the master die. (The master die is used to make working hubs, which in turn are used to make working dies, which are used to strike coins.)

The original Franklin half dollar master die was employed from 1948 through 1959. It deteriorated over the years to the point of losing all of the hair details on Franklin's head in the mid- to late 1950s. U.S. Mint engravers reworked the master die, resulting in most of the details of the original obverse design being restored beginning with 1960 Franklin halves. However, the die rework did not fully restore the lines on the Liberty Bell on the coin's reverse, thus retaining a weakness into the last four years of issue.

The challenge for graders is to know the die characteristics in order to properly grade Franklin half dollars.

More than half of Tomaska's book is devoted to a date-by-date analysis of the various characteristics of regular issue Franklin halves. He also provides an in-depth date analysis for grading Proof Franklin half dollars.

Franklin half dollars enjoyed wide circulation from the first year of issue in 1948 through the mid-1950s. Due to its buying power, few were put aside as collectibles. In 1948 a loaf of bread cost 14 cents and a gallon of gas was 26 cents. Fewer Franklins circulated in 1963, the last year of issue, but the half dollar was still worth taking to the grocery store, where a loaf of bread cost 21 cents, and a half dollar could purchase two gallons of gasoline.

When silver approached $50 per ounce in 1980, circulated silver Franklin half dollars shared the fate of many older circulated U.S. silver coins. They were sold for melt value, which was many multiples of the coin's face value. Consequently, most Franklin half dollars that trade in the collector market today tend to be About Uncirculated 58 to Mint State 63. Higher Mint State grades are elusive because of the number of contact marks present on most circulation strikes.

Surface preservation – the condition of the surfaces on both sides of the coin – is especially important. The Franklin portrait is centered on the obverse with a large field on either side. Contact marks in the fields are found on most circulation strikes, evidence of where the coin has collided with other coins or objects. Tiny scratches referred to as "hairlines" created by abrasive substances or material used in cleaning are also commonly found in the fields. Imperfections may also be evident that were created on the coin's surface during various stages of its manufacture.

In analyzing the state of the surfaces of a Franklin half dollar, one must weigh the visual impact of these imperfections and weigh the degree of severity and whether the locations of the imperfections seriously detract from the coin's overall appearance.

In the Franklin half dollar map RED is considered Worst (Average x 4), ORANGE is Bad (Average x 2), YELLOW is Average, GREEN is Better (Average x 1/2) and BLUE is Best (Average x 1/4). A mark in the red area is about eight times more serious than if the same mark is in the green area. The worst places on the obverse for a mark or scratch are on Franklin's face and the date. On the reverse, the worst places for scratches and marks are on the Liberty Bell. (Copyright 1990, HeritageCoins.com.)

Design high points on the obverse and reverse of the Franklin half dollar are highlighted in red. High points on the obverse are on Franklin's head near the beginning of his hairline, his cheekbone and the fold of his cheek line to the jawbone, the curl of hair behind his ear, the top of his jacket and the center of the bottom portion of the bust. On the reverse, high points are on both sides of the lower portion of the beam from which the Liberty Bell is hanging, on the straps holding the crown of the bell, in the center of the top decorative belts (lines), and on the lower belts (lines) on both sides of the crack in the bell, and on the breast of the small eagle to the right of the bell.

VG-8: Well worn overall. Obverse: Franklin's head is weak with most hair details from temple to ear worn smooth. Letters in legends and date are bold. Designer's initials and ear are visible; rim is complete. Reverse: Entire bell is worn and very little detail remains. Straps on beam are weak but are visible. The rim merges with letters of legends.

F-12: Moderate to heavy wear evenly over entire coin. Obverse: Details of hair visible only on side and back of head. Designer's initials clearly visible but weak. Part of cheek is flat from wear. Reverse: Parts of straps on beam almost smooth. Most of lower lines on bell are worn smooth. Rim is full.

VF-20: Wear is even and moderate. Obverse: 75 percent of strands of hair visible. Some hair detail visible around the ear. Cheek lightly worn but bold. Reverse: Bell is worn but bold. Although most details of beam are visible, wear evident on beam. Lines flat across bottom of bell near crack.

VF-30: Wear is light and all major features are sharp. Obverse: Spotty wear evident on jaw, cheek and on hair at shoulder and behind the ear. Reverse: 50 percent of line details at bottom of bell worn smooth. Straps of beam visible. Wear evident on bell lettering, but some detail visible.

EF-40: Light wear on highest points of design elements. Obverse: Wear discernable on high points of cheek, hair behind ear and on shoulder. Reverse: Slight wear on high points of beam straps and lines on bottom of bell, but design elements clearly defined and partially separated. Lettering on center of bell is worn away.

EF-45: Very light wear on highest points. Half of Mint luster still present. Obverse: Slight wear on cheek and hair behind ear and along the shoulder. Hair details on the back of the head are sharp. Reverse: High points of straps around the beam are slightly worn. Lines on bottom of bell are clearly defined and separated, but are worn.

AU-50: Seventy-five percent of Mint luster remains. Traces of wear on highest design points. Obverse: Traces of wear on cheek, hair left of the ear and on shoulder. Reverse: Traces of wear detectable on lettering in center of bell and on rim at bottom of bell.

AU-55: Nearly all of Mint luster remains. Slight traces of wear. Obverse: Traces of wear on highest points of cheek and hair left of ear. Reverse: Trace of wear evident on highest points of lettering on the bell.

AU-58: Some signs of abrasions evident. Obverse: Very slight wear on high points of cheek, shoulder and hair left of the ear. Reverse: Very slight wear detectable on straps around the beam, on the lines of the bell and lettering on the bell.

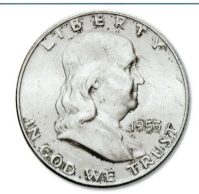

MS-60: No traces of wear detectable. May lack full Mint luster. Surfaces may be dull, spotted or heavily toned. May have heavy contact marks in all areas and noticeable patches of hairlines. Poor general eye appeal.

MS-61: No traces of wear permitted. May have a few heavy or numerous light contact marks in prime focal areas and secondary areas. May have noticeable hairline scratches on surfaces. Generally has unattractive eye appeal.

MS-62: Uncirculated, but may have a few distracting contact marks in prime focal areas and in secondary areas. May have a few scattered hairline scratches. Luster may be impaired or original. Eye appeal is generally acceptable.

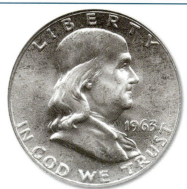

MS-63: May have contact marks and minor blemishes in prime focal areas and a few hairlines. Must have attractive Mint luster and be rather attractive to the eye.

MS-64: May have light scattered contact marks, with few in prime focal areas. May have a few scattered or small patches of hairline scratches in secondary areas. Mint luster must be average, full original. Overall eye appeal should be pleasing.

MS-65: No trace of wear. Nearly perfect except for some small blemishes in secondary areas. May have a few scattered hairline scratches. Luster must be fully original. Eye appeal should be very pleasing.

CoinWorld

174

Kennedy Half Dollar

With a diameter of 30.61 millimeters or 1.21 inches, the Kennedy half dollar is the largest current U.S. coin in circulation, although new issues do not circulate widely. From 2002 through 2005, the U.S. Mint produced circulation strikes only for the collector market rather than for general use in commerce.

The Kennedy half dollar's size and availability since 1964 render it highly collectible. And those two aspects also make it an ideal coin for new or beginning collectors to use in gaining an understanding of the basics of coin grading.

U.S. Mint Chief Sculptor-Engraver Gilroy Roberts prepared the obverse left-facing portrait of John F. Kennedy for the half dollar coin from the portrait he had rendered for Kennedy's presidential medal, which was issued before the president was assassinated. Open fields surround the large portrait with the LIBERTY legend spread around the rim. The reverse features the presidential seal, with the heraldic eagle as its main design element. Independence Hall is featured on the two-year (1975 and 1976) Bicentennial reverse of the Kennedy half dollar.

Due to availability, it is possible to assemble a year and Mint mark collection of circulation strike Kennedy half dollars in Uncirculated condition for a relatively modest sum.

Critical to determining whether the coin is Uncirculated is inspecting the surfaces for evidence of wear.

Look at the high points of the design to detect wear. High points on the Kennedy half dollar are easy to spot. On the obverse the design high points are on Kennedy's cheek and jaw, on his ear, on the hair below the part, and on the center portion of the bottom of his neck. On the reverse, the design high points are noticeable on the eagle's neck, the back portion of its head, the eagle's center tail feather and the center arrow the eagle is holding in his left talon. Also, early signs of wear can be detected on the three center clouds above the rays in the presidential seal.

These are the areas where wear from circulation is most likely to appear first. However, grading experts also caution that these are the same areas that tend to lack detail if the coin is weakly struck or if it was struck from worn dies.

Begin your Kennedy half dollar inspection by carefully observing it, tilting the coin back and forth to see how the luster flows over the design high points. The tilting action helps you to detect differences in the luster. On the Uncirculated coin, the full luster will roll over the high points. On an AU coin the luster is broken and can be seen without magnification. It does not take long to discern slight wear, which is actually the displacement of metal.

A couple of important points to remember: Roll contact marks are common on Mint State Kennedy half dollars – whether 1964 90 percent silver strikes, the 1965 to 1970 40 percent silver versions, or later copper-nickel clad strikes – and slight "friction" on the high points or in the fields is also evident. Such is the result of coins rubbing against each other in rolls or bags as they were packaged for distribution at the U.S. Mint. If the metal is not disturbed and the luster is intact, the coin is deemed Mint State.

Location and severity of imperfections are keys to determining the status of the Kennedy half dollar's surface. The worst place for a mark or scratch is the middle of Kennedy's cheek, the focal point of the coin. Contact marks are also often found on Kennedy's neck, and sometimes on various areas of his head. The large field seems to be a gathering place for contact marks and hairline scratches, all of which can take away from the overall eye appeal.

Although marks and other imperfections are sometimes found on rims of the Kennedy half dollar, they are less detracting and less noticeable. Because the rim is the least important part of the coin's total design, marks on the rim do not significantly lower the grade.

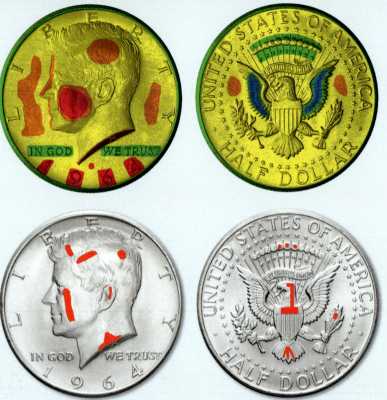

In the Kennedy half dollar map RED is considered Worst (Average x 4), ORANGE is Bad (Average x 2), YELLOW is Average, GREEN is Better (Average x 1/2) and BLUE is Best (Average x 1/4). A mark in the red area is about eight times more serious than if the same mark is in the green area. The worst places on the obverse for a mark or scratch are on Kennedy's cheek and digits of the date. On the reverse, the worst places for scratches and marks are in the fields under the eagle's outspread wings. (Copyright 2005, HeritageCoins.com.)

AU-50   AU-55   AU-58

Expert graders suggest beginners use magnifying glasses "at least as large as the coin you are grading," in order to keep contact marks and wear in perspective. Too much magnification can be confusing. For example, the cheek areas of the AU-50, AU-55, and AU-58 graded Kennedy halves shown were photographed using a 10-power digital microscope under the same lighting conditions. The close-up views, and above, are virtually indistinguishable for grading purposes, whereas wear and contact marks are readily discernable when inspecting the coins without using magnification.

Design high points on the obverse and reverse of the Kennedy half dollar are highlighted in red. The highest points on the obverse are on Kennedy's cheek, his hair near the part, inside the ear and at center base of his neck. Reverse high points are the centers of the 13 clouds between the rays, the eagle's head and neck, the center of the shield, the lower center tail feathers, and arrows in the eagle's left talons.

AU-50: Wear evident on the cheek, jawbone and hair below the part as well as slight wear in the field on the obverse. On the reverse, wear is detectable on the central tail feathers, top of the shield and right side of eagle's head.

AU-55: Only a trace of wear shows on the highest points of the obverse – cheek, jawbone and hair below the part. On the reverse, a trace of wear is visible on the central tail feather. Almost all of the Mint luster remains.

AU-58: Some light traces of wear visible on high points of cheek, jawbone, center of neck and hair below part on obverse. Abrasions evident on the bundle of arrows, center tail feather, and right wing tip on reverse.

MS-60: Uncirculated coin with no trace of wear. May have large number of contact marks, may have dull, impaired luster, and may be noticeably spotted or stained.

MS-61: No traces of wear. Numerous contact marks easily visible throughout coin, including face and neck of Kennedy. May have numerous patches of light hairline scratches, may have impaired luster.

MS-62: Fewer obvious contact marks on design devices and in the fields, no traces of wear, and average luster.

MS-63: Uncirculated coin with attractive Mint luster, but with noticeable detracting contact marks or minor blemishes.

MS-64: No trace of wear; seems perfect except for scattered contact marks that become obvious with careful, second look. Attractive luster and overall eye appeal.

MS-65: No trace of wear; nearly perfect except for a few small blemishes. Has full Mint luster, but may be unevenly toned or lightly finger-marked. A few barely noticeable nicks or marks may be present.

Morgan Dollar

The Morgan dollar is the most popularly collected coin in the U.S. series. Its large diameter – 1.5 inches (38.1 millimeters) – and large obverse portrait suggest it should be easy to grade. But the intricate detail U.S. Mint Engraver George T. Morgan created in this left-facing, large head of Liberty plus design modifications over the years of issue present some formidable grading challenges.

First, one must be aware of the design modifications because they affect grading. The obverse design used from 1878 through 1904, though essentially the same as the one-year issue of 1921, was struck in higher relief. The result is that wear on the hair above Liberty's ear (a key design high point) looks different on the 1921 lower relief strikes. There are three primary styles of reverses. The eagle's breast is rounded on most issues struck from 1878 to 1904, but it is noticeably flat on some dollars dated 1878 through 1880. The 1921 reverse is known for its weak strike on the eagle's breast. These characteristics must be kept in mind, particularly when grading circulated Morgan dollars.

Morgan dollars were struck in large quantities at the "mother" Mint in Philadelphia and at four Branch Mint facilities: San Francisco, Carson City, New Orleans and Denver. Most did not circulate and were stored in Mint-sewn bags at various Treasury facilities for decades. Hundreds of millions were melted in 1918, with remaining supplies gradually dispersed as the public redeemed silver certificates for the coins, until redemption ended in 1968. The last dollars, mostly Carson City Mint dollars, were sold at premiums in the 1970s.

Availability of so many "cartwheels" spawned a collecting and research revolution in the U.S. marketplace. No other single series today is so widely researched, resulting in more than 2,000 die varieties and stages having been identified and codified, in the major reference, *The Comprehensive Catalog and Encyclopedia of Morgan and Peace Dollars* by Leroy C. Van Allen and A. George Mallis, now in its sixth edition, and subsequent to the publication of that book.

Our grading discussion necessarily focuses on general aspects of the series. Keep in mind that the obverse is by far the most important side of a Morgan dollar. It generally accounts for 75 to 90 percent of the grade.

Grading specialists recommend grading Morgan dollars without the use of magnification, using a magnifier only to check details for possible signs of wear.

Morgan dollars with the slightest wear will evidence "gray areas" at the high points of the design. Tilt the coin from side to side and then slightly on the up-and-down axis. On the obverse, look for a grayish cast on the hair above Liberty's ear. On the reverse, check for the grayish cast at the center of the eagle's breast. The grayish cast is an indication of a definite loss of luster, which is the first sign of wear.

Beginning collectors are sometimes confused by the fact that some flatly struck About Uncirculated Morgan dollars show less detail than some Extremely Fine dollars. The AU coin with less detail than the EF is exhibiting weak strike. All of the minting facilities had striking problems, but New Orleans produced the weakest strikes. It is important to identify the striking characteristics of each minting facility. Wayne Miller's *Morgan and Peace Dollar Textbook*, published in 1982, is still the standard reference work on Morgan dollars. It details the characteristics and the idiosyncrasies of each date and Mint mark in the series.

While mastering the basics of grading circulated Morgan dollars can be accomplished in a short period, mastering the art of grading Mint State Morgans is a much more complex and time-consuming matter. It entails being able to identify on a date-by-date basis the standard for luster for each issuing Mint, since luster is generally agreed upon as the single most important factor in grading Uncirculated Morgan dollars. In addition, one must be able to evaluate the location and severity of contact marks, scratches, nicks and hairlines on the coin's surface. After factoring in strike, overall eye appeal must be given consideration. Viewing Morgan dollars graded by the leading grading services can help in learning the characteristics of the many coins in the vast domain of Morgan dollars.

In the Morgan dollar map RED is considered Worst (Average x 4), ORANGE is Bad (Average x 2), YELLOW is Average, GREEN is Better (Average x 1/2) and BLUE is Best (Average x 1/4). A mark in the red area is about eight times more serious than if the same mark is in the green area. The worst places on the obverse for a mark or scratch are on the lower half of Liberty's face and the date. On the reverse, the worst places for scratches and marks are on the eagle's breast feathers. (Copyright 1990, HeritageCoins.com.)

Design high points on the obverse and reverse of the Morgan dollar are highlighted in red. The highest points on the obverse are on Liberty's cheekbone, eyebrow, center curl below B in LIBERTY, hair above ear, center of third hair curl at base of neck, lower portion of curl in peak of Liberty cap, and lower crease in cap. Reverse high points are on the eagle's neck and center breast feathers.

G-4: Design devices, legends visible but may be faint in spots. Obverse hair well worn, little detail remains. Date, letters and design clearly outlined, rim full. Reverse eagle worn almost flat but outlined. Design elements and legends smooth, but visible. Rim full.

VG-8: Well worn, with design devices clear but flat. Lacks details. Obverse hair worn smooth. All letters, date clear. Cotton bolls flat, leaves merging in spots. Half of reverse eagle's right wing and a third of left wing smooth. All wreath leaves worn. Rim complete.

F-12: Entire design clear, bold. Obverse hairline clearly defined. Lower two cotton leaves smooth but distinct from cap. Some wheat grains merging. Cotton bolls flat but two lines clear. Quarter of eagle's right wing and edge of left wing on reverse smooth. Head, neck, breast flat.

VF-20: Light to moderate even wear. All major features sharp. On obverse, smooth spots visible from forehead hair to ear. Cotton leaves heavily worn, separated. Wear on wheat grains. Reverse wreath leaves well worn. Eagle's breast smooth, few feathers show on head.

VF-30: Wear on obverse visible on high points of hair from forehead to ear. Some strands visible in hair above ear. Some smooth areas on cotton leaves, top of cotton bolls. On reverse, wear visible on wreath leaves, wing tips. Few feathers visible on breast, head.

EF-40: Very light wear on highest points. Wear shows on obverse hair above date, forehead, and ear. Light wear on cheek. Lines in hair well detailed. Flat spots on cotton leaf edges. Reverse eagle breast feathers almost all absent. Leg tops, wing tips, head feathers show wear.

EF-45: Wear slight on hair above date, forehead, ear. Lines in hair detailed, sharp. Slight flat spots on cotton leaf edges. Minute wear on cheek. On reverse, high points of breast slightly worn. Wear visible on leg tops, right wing tip. Talons slightly flat. Half of Mint luster present.

AU-50: Traces of wear on hair above eye, ear, cotton leaf edges, upper folds of cap. Partial detail on cotton bolls. No luster on cheek. On reverse, traces of wear on eagle's breast, leg tops, wing tips and talons. Three-quarters of Mint luster present. Surface abrasions and contacts marks noticeable.

AU-55: On obverse, slight traces of wear evident on hair above ear, eye, cotton leaf edges, upper cap fold. Luster fading from cheek. On reverse, slight trace of wear on eagle's breast, leg tops, talons. Most of Mint luster present. Light surface abrasions, contact marks.

AU-58: Small trace of wear on highest points. On obverse, some signs of wear on hair above ear, cotton leaf edges, bolls, upper cap fold. On reverse, some signs of wear on eagle's breast, tops of legs.

MS-60: Heavy contact marks on the cheek, numerous light marks in the left field and the neck. Luster is good, and strike is above average for an 1887-O.

MS-61: Very noticeable contact marks, including reed marks to the left of the ear and long cuts to the left of the chin. Luster is average, strike is sharp.

MS-62: Numerous contact marks on the cheek, neck, and fields, but none that are heavy or disfiguring. Luster is original, strike is sharp.

M-63: Contact marks are lighter and less concentrated. Luster is original, strike is sharp. Overall eye appeal is pleasing.

MS-64: Contact marks are lighter and more scattered. Cheek reasonably clean, with no heavy marks or hairlines. Luster is original, strike is sharp. Overall eye appeal is very pleasing.

MS-65: Contact marks are very light, with none that distract the eye. The light contact marks on the cheek, neck and left field are minor and separated. Luster is full and original, strike is sharp. Eye appeal is excellent.

MS-66: Contact marks are minimal. The cheek is nearly perfect, with a small grouping of marks to the left of the chin being the main blemish. Luster is full and original, strike is sharp. Eye appeal is excellent.

MS-67: Contact marks are virtually nonexistent. (The only marks allowed for the MS-67 grade must be small and difficult to see.) Luster is full and original, strike is full. Eye appeal is exceptional.

Peace Dollar

The Peace dollar is an attractive and affordable coin to collect because only 24 coins are needed to complete a date and Mint mark collection and it is widely available in the marketplace in the various grades.

Sculptor Anthony deFrancisci's design for the large (1.5-inch) diameter 90 percent silver dollar features on the obverse a portrait of Liberty facing left, wearing a needle-like radiant headdress. On the reverse, an eagle (symbolic of the United States) stands atop a ledge looking into a rising sun (symbolic of a new day) clutching an olive branch (symbolic of peace) in its talons.

One aspect that often confuses new collectors is the spelling of "trust" in the motto. DeFrancisci used Latin style letters for the required motto IN GOD WE TRVST. He used a "V" instead of the "U." The word TRVST appears on all Peace dollars dated 1921 to 1935 to the right of the base of Liberty's neck. Standing alone gives the word more prominence. Hence, many people notice the spelling as one of the first memorable aspects of the design, and wonder whether they have an error coin.

The name "Peace dollar" derives from its authorization as commemorative of the signing of the peace treaty between the United States and Germany at the end of World War I. The idea for the Peace dollar originated with Farran Zerbe, a coin collector and historian for the American Numismatic Association. Zerbe proposed the issuance of a circulating coin to commemorate the peace in a research paper presented at the ANA's 1920 annual convention in Chicago. The idea found legislative backers, but the proposal failed to gain passage in Congress. Secretary of the Treasury Andrew W. Mellon saved the idea by approving a design change for the standard silver dollar, resurrected in 1921 after an end in production in 1904.

DeFrancisci's design was rendered in high relief in 1921, and then was changed to a somewhat lower relief beginning in 1922. The relief resulted in striking problems for much of the series. Successfully grading Peace dollars requires study of the striking characteristics of each year and Mint mark.

Peace dollars struck in high relief invariably display weakness in the central areas of the obverse and reverse. Liberty's hair may be extremely flat and the eagle may be missing central wing feathers on some of the high relief strikes. Specialists note that even on well-struck Peace dollars, Liberty's highest curls and the tops of the eagle's wing feathers are often slightly incomplete. Also, the eagle's wing feathers just above his right leg are often incomplete. Generally, Philadelphia Mint strikes are better than Denver Mint strikes.

The San Francisco Mint wins the prize for the poorest strikes of Peace dollars.

Peace dollars are found with many contact marks – even the Uncirculated specimens. Contact marks are common on Liberty's hair, face and neck as well as the field. On the reverse, contact marks are routinely encountered on the eagle as well as the field. Specialists note that beginning graders tend to count the number of marks and assign a grade, which they say is a major mistake. They contend that luster is important and rank failure to recognize substandard luster as the most common error made by those first attempting to grade Peace dollars. Peace dollars almost always grade lower than what the beginner anticipates because of deficient luster. Cleaning and gross overdipping are two common causes for substandard luster.

Many Peace dollars lack eye appeal. Few exhibit toning and luster variations are limited. Often the highest graded Peace dollars are those struck at the Philadelphia and Denver Mint that display satin to frosty luster, with little to no toning.

Professional graders suggest that the best way to become truly knowledgeable in grading Peace dollars is to view as many certified examples as possible to get a feel for the idiosyncrasies and tendencies of the dates and Mint marks for the series.

In the Peace dollar map RED is considered Worst (Average x 4), ORANGE is Bad (Average x 2), YELLOW is Average, GREEN is Better (Average x 1/2) and BLUE is Best (Average x 1/4). A mark in the red area is about eight times more serious than if the same mark is in the green area. The worst places on the obverse for a mark or scratch are on Liberty's face, neck and the date. On the reverse, the worst places for scratches and marks are on the eagle's wings and body. (Copyright 1990, HeritageCoins.com.)

High points of the design are the best places to detect wear. Peace dollar obeverse high points are on Liberty's cheek and on the center portion of the bottom of her neck. On the reverse, the design high points are on the center of the eagle's wing. (Copyright 1990, HeritageCoins.com.)

P-01: Obverse and reverse designs barely discernable. All legends and numerals worn completely away.

F-15: Moderate to heavy, even wear, but entire design is clear and bold. All hair around face smooth, rays show trace of wear. Reverse feathers on right leg worn away. Parts of legends weak but readable.

VF-20: On obverse, very little hair detail visible around face, wear on upper wave. Hair above ear worn, but some single strands clear. On reverse, wing detail worn but three horizontal lines of feather layers show. Leg feathers, neck flat. Slight wear on motto and talons.

VF-30: Hair details weak around face on obverse. Light wear on upper hair wave; hair above ear worn but single strands defined. On reverse, motto shows trace of wear. Right wing feather details weak. Wear on leg feathers, neck.

EF-40: Partial Mint luster. Slight flattening on high points of hair, most strands separate. Slight wear on face and neck. On reverse, wear on head behind eye and top of neck. Flat spots on central wing, leg feathers.

EF-45: 50 percent of Mint luster remains. On obverse, light wear on hair around face but most strands visible. Lower neck lightly worn. On reverse, top of neck, head behind eye exhibit slight wear as do central wing and leg feathers.

AU-50: 75 percent of Mint luster present. Noticeable contact marks, surface abrasions. Traces of wear visible on neck, hair over ear, above forehead and cheek on obverse; head and highpoints of feathers on right wing on reverse.

AU-55: Trace of wear on hair over ear, above forehead and on cheek on obverse. Trace of wear on high points of feathers on reverse. Most of Mint luster remains. Light contact marks, surface abrasions.

AU-58: Small trace of wear on one or more of the high points of design. No detracting contact marks in prime and secondary focal areas. Attractive eye appeal; nearly full Mint luster.

MS-60: Uncirculated coin with heavy contact marks in all areas and noticeable hairline scratches on the surfaces. Luster can be original or impaired. Generally poor eye appeal.

MS-61: Generally unattractive Uncirculated coin. May have a few heavy or many light contact marks in prime and secondary areas; noticeable patch or continuous hairline scratches.

MS-62: May have distracting contact marks in prime and secondary areas; may have scattered or noticeable patch of hairline scratches. Original Mint luster may be impaired.

MS-63: Uncirculated with attractive Mint luster, which may be slightly impaired. May have distracting contact marks in prime focal areas and a few scattered or small patch of hairline scratches.

MS-64: Average, full original luster. May have light, scattered contact marks with a few in prime focal areas. May have a few, small hairline scratches. Pleasing eye appeal.

MS-65: No trace of wear. May have a few light, minute contact marks. Must have full original Mint luster. Very pleasing eye appeal; may exhibit uneven toning.

Eisenhower Dollar

The Eisenhower dollar, popularly known as the Ike dollar, is the last large-size dollar coin struck for circulation by the U.S. Mint. Its 38.1-millimeter (1.5-inch) diameter and obverse portrait with a large open field render it among the easiest U.S. coins to grade and the least complicated of the dollar denomination. That being said, the low relief and sometime poor striking quality of the copper-nickel clad versions struck for circulation can be tricky to grade.

U.S. Mint Chief Engraver Frank Gasparro chose to depict the great general Dwight David Eisenhower in a left-facing profile (head and neck) in his early 60s with a receding hairline, much as he looked when elected president in late 1952.

The first reverse, based on the Apollo 11 mission patch, features a bald eagle landing on the crater-pocked surface of the Moon with an olive branch clutched in its talons. In the background, the Earth is rising over the Moon's horizon.

The second reverse (on dollar coins dual dated 1776-1976 commemorating the nation's Bicentennial) was designed by Dennis R. Williams and depicts the Liberty Bell superimposed on the Moon. The Liberty Bell-Moon reverse, featuring the two design devices, has a large, open field.

Because the Ike dollars did not widely circulate, they are not often found in grades below About Uncirculated 50. Often, AU-58 graded coins will have more eye appeal than the lower Mint State grades because the coin may have fewer contact marks and imperfections. However, the AU-58 designation signals that the slightest bit of wear has been detected on the high points of the coin's design elements.

Use incandescent lighting for grading Eisenhower dollars and inspect the surface of the coins with your eyes, without magnification, tilting and rotating the coin, looking for a contrast of luster between the high points and the rest of the coin.

If you detect a contrast of luster between the high points and the rest of the coin, use a loupe or hand-held magnifier of up to a 7-power magnification to inspect for rubbing. Abrasions on the high points drop the grade to circulated.

Contact marks are permitted in the Uncirculated grades, but their number and location help to determine where the grade will ultimately land on the Mint State scale. The more contact marks, the lower the grade, especially if they detract from the overall eye appeal. The large open fields on the Eisenhower dollar provide relatively little area for contact marks to hide.

Most of the circulation strikes of the Eisenhower copper-nickel clad dollars are found with contact marks on the face, neck and head of the portrait and well as in the field of the obverse. Similarly, both reverses of the copper-nickel clad versions are prone to show contact marks, although somewhat less than the obverse. The 40 percent silver versions and the Proof copper-nickel clad issues exhibit few marks because they were produced with more care and were issued in sealed sets.

Many of the Eisenhower copper-nickel clad dollars were struck in low relief and exhibit weak strikes. On the obverse, the high points on the hair above the ear and about halfway between the ear and the top of the head appear incomplete. Other areas that may be affected include the eyebrow, the cheekbone, the line of the jaw, ear, nose and chin. On the Eagle Landing reverse, weakness of strike is sometimes seen on the eagle, the olive branch, the Moon and lettering in the legends. On the Liberty Bell-Moon reverse, strike problem areas include the upper bell lines and lettering between and below the upper bell lines, on the left side of the middle bell lines, and on the Moon.

Most of the Eisenhower 40 percent silver dollars are well struck and many are fully struck. Most have exceptional eye appeal because they have great luster, exhibit minimal marks and were protected by the holders in which they were issued. However, finding copper-nickel clad issues with great eye appeal can be a challenge because few are encountered that are both well struck and exhibit few contact marks.

Eisenhower Dollar

In the Eisenhower half dollar map RED is considered Worst (Average x 4), ORANGE is Bad (Average x 2), YELLOW is Average, GREEN is Better (Average x 1/2) and BLUE is Best (Average x 1/4). A mark in the red area is about eight times more serious than if the same mark is in the green area. The worst places on the obverse for a mark or scratch are on Eisenhower's cheekbone, the Mint mark and date. On the reverse, the worst places for scratches and marks are on the eagle's head and breast feathers near the eagle's outspread left wing. (Copyright 2005, HeritageCoins.com.)

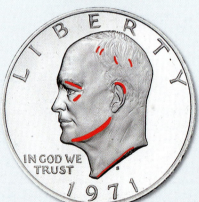

Design high points, shown in red, on the obverse of the Eisenhower dollar are on the portrait, along the jawbone, on the cheek, base of the neck, along the eyebrow and on top of the ear. High points of the Eagle Landing reverse are on the top of eagle's right wing and at top of eagle's left wing, on the eagle's head behind the eye, eagle's right talon and on feathers at top of eagle's left leg. On the Liberty Bell-Moon reverse the design high points include the right and left side of beam, upper and lower belts (lines) on the bell, and right portion of the Moon.

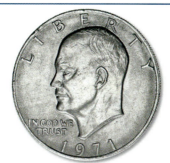

AU-50: Light wear visible on high points of the design. Half of the luster remains. Obverse: Light wear evident along the jawbone, on the cheek, base of the neck, along the eyebrow, and on top of the ear. Hair is sharp and detailed. Eagle Landing reverse: Light wear evident on top of eagle's right wing and at top of eagle's left wing, on eagle's head behind the eye, eagle's right talon and on feathers at top of eagle's left leg. Liberty Bell-Moon reverse: Wear evident on right and left side of beam, upper and lower belts (lines) on the bell, and right portion of the moon.

AU-55: Trace of wear visible on design high points. Three quarters of luster remains. Obverse: Slight traces of wear visible along the jawbone, on the cheek and at the center of the neck. Eagle Landing reverse: Slight trace of wear on high points of feathers in eagle's wings and on top of eagle's left leg. Liberty Bell-Moon reverse: Slight traces of wear visible on upper and lower bell lines and on right side of moon.

AU-58: Slightest trace of wear detectable on highest points of design elements. Nearly all of the Mint luster present. Obverse: Some signs of abrasion visible on high points of cheek, jawbone, center of neck, edge of bust, and head. Eagle Landing reverse: Slightest traces of abrasion detectable on high points of ridges and feathers on eagle's wings and legs. Liberty Bell-Moon reverse: Slightest trace of abrasion visible on upper and lower bell lines and right side of the moon.

MS-60: Absolutely no trace of wear permitted. Mint luster may be unattractive, dull or washed out. May have large, detracting contact marks or damage spots. Rim nicks may be present. Eye appeal is very poor.

MS-61: Mint luster may be noticeably impaired or diminished. Clusters of large and small contacts marks visible on surface of coin. Hairline scratches may be very noticeable. Scuff marks may be present on major design elements. Small rim nicks and striking or planchet defects may show. Surface quality may be poor and overall eye appeal is somewhat unattractive.

MS-62: Mint luster may be dull or impaired. Clusters of small marks may be present on surfaces and a few large marks or nicks are permitted in the prime focal areas. Hairline scratches are generally very noticeable and large scuff marks may be present on major design elements. Strike, rim and planchet quality may be noticeably below average. Eye appeal overall is generally acceptable.

MS-63: Slight impairment of Mint luster detectable. A few scattered heavy marks and numerous small contact marks permitted. Small hairline scratches visible without magnification. Several scuff marks or detracting defects may be present on design elements or in the fields. General quality of the coin is about average. Overall, the coin is rather attractive.

MS-64: Mint luster and strike are average. Several groups of small contact marks permitted as well as one or two moderately heavy marks. One or two small patches of hairline scratches may be visible under low magnification. Light scuff marks or defects may be detectable on design elements or in the fields. Displays attractive quality and eye appeal is pleasing.

MS-65: Mint luster and strike are attractive and of high quality for the date and Mint facility at which coin was struck. A few, small and scattered contact marks or two larger marks permitted. One or two small patches of hairline scratches visible under magnification. Light scuff marks may be detectable on design high points. Quality overall is above average and overall eye appeal is very pleasing.

Eisenhower Dollar

MS-66: Quality of strike is above average. Full, original Mint luster must be present. No more than two or three noticeable minor contact marks permitted. A few very light hairline scratches may show under magnification or one or two light scuff marks permitted on major design elements or in the fields. Eye appeal must be very pleasing and above average for the date and Mint.

MS-67: Strike is sharp for the date and Mint at which it was struck. Full, original Mint luster present. Three to four very small contact marks and one other noticeable but not detracting mark permitted. One or two small single hairline scratches may show under magnification, or one or two partially hidden scuff marks or flaws may be detectable. Eye appeal is exceptional.

MS-68: Original full Mint luster present. Strike is sharp for the date and the Mint facility that produced it. No more than four, light, scattered, contact marks or flaws permitted. No visible hairline scratches or scuff marks permitted. Eye appeal must be exceptional.

PF-69: Virtually as struck with minuscule imperfections. Nearly full strike.

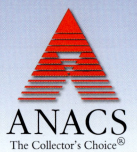

Susan B. Anthony Dollar

The public's rejection of the Anthony dollar is a boon to collectors. Most Anthony dollars exist in Uncirculated condition. But even those encountered in circulation exist in high states of preservation.

Two factors beyond low circulation contribute to the surprisingly nice condition of the coins. First, all four years of issue are made of the hard and durable silver-colored alloy of two outer layers of 75 percent copper, 25 percent nickel bonded to a core of pure copper. Second, the obverse design was intentionally rendered in low relief to ensure a long circulation life.

U.S. Mint Chief Engraver Frank Gasparro worked from photographs to depict Susan B. Anthony in a right-facing, large portrait at approximately age 50, with her hair pulled back in a bun. Although the coin is round, it has an 11-sided inner border. Using the LIBERTY legend over the top of Anthony's portrait and the date below, Gasparro incorporated six stars on the right and seven stars on the left of the border to connect the legend and date. He placed the Mint mark on the left side above Anthony's shoulder and his initials on the right side below her shoulder and above the first star. The required IN GOD WE TRUST motto is at chin level on the right side.

As directed by Congress, Gasparro adapted the first reverse he created for the larger Eisenhower dollar to the smaller canvas of the SBA dollar. Based on the Apollo 11 mission patch, it features a bald eagle landing on the crater-pocked surface of the Moon with an olive branch clutched in its talons. In the background, the Earth is rising over the Moon's horizon.

The greatest grading challenge is spotting wear on the high points of the design so as to be able to distinguish between About Uncirculated 58 and the first level of Uncirculated, Mint State 60.

Obverse high points include Anthony's cheekbone, her hair in the center of her head above the ear, and the collar button. On the reverse, high points are on the eagle's head and neck and the feathers on the top edges of his wings and on his legs. (Mint officials said the high relief on the top of the eagle's head and wings was intended to give the visually impaired reference points in order to tactilely identify the coin.)

The design high points are areas where the wear from circulation will appear first.

Grading specialists suggest using incandescent lighting for grading Anthony dollars. Also, they suggest inspecting the surface of the coin with your eyes, without magnification, tilting and rotating the coin, looking for a contrast of luster between the high points and the rest of the coin.

If you detect a contrast of luster between the high points and the rest of the coin, use a loupe or hand-held magnifier of up to a 7-power magnification to inspect for rubbing. Abrasions on the high points drop the grade to circulated.

Contact marks are permitted in the Uncirculated grades, but their number and location help to determine where the grade will ultimately land on the Mint State scale. The more contact marks, the lower the grade, especially if they detract from the overall eye appeal. Uncirculated Anthony dollars retrieved from new rolls and Mint-sewn bags tend to exist in the mid-Mint State ranges up to MS-65.

On the obverse contact marks and other abrasions are primarily found on Anthony's face, hair and neck. On the reverse, the eagle's body constitutes the prime focal area for contact marks.

Most Anthony dollars are fully struck. Areas of weakness, when found, tend to be on the hair around Anthony's ear on the obverse and the central part of the eagle's body on the reverse.

Most Anthony dollars exhibit satiny to slightly frosty surfaces, with very few rising to the level of very frosty. Semi-prooflike and prooflike surfaces are rare.

Very few Anthony dollars rise to the level of having spectacular eye appeal.

In the Susan B. Anthony dollar map RED is considered Worst (Average x 4), ORANGE is Bad (Average x 2), YELLOW is Average, GREEN is Better (Average x 1/2) and BLUE is Best (Average x 1/4). A mark in the red area is about eight times more serious than if the same mark is in the green area. The worst places on the obverse for a mark or scratch are on Anthony's cheek and jaw and the date. On the reverse, the worst places for scratches and marks are on breast feathers near the eagle's outspread left wing, and fields above the eagle's head and below the eagle's left wing. (Copyright 2005, HeritageCoins.com.)

Design high points for the Anthony dollar are shown in red. Design high points on the obverse include Anthony's cheekbone, her hair in the center of her head above the ear, and the collar button. On the reverse, high points are on the eagle's head and neck and on the feathers on the top edges of his wings and on his legs.

AU-55: Small trace of wear visible on design high points. Obverse: Trace of wear detectible on highest points of Susan B. Anthony's cheekbone, on her hair in the center of her head above the ear and on the collar button. Reverse: Trace of wear shows on high points of the eagle's neck and the feathers on the top edges of his wings and on his legs. Almost all of the Mint luster is present.

AU-58: Slightest trace of wear shows on design high points. Obverse: Some signs of abrasion detectible on the high points of SBA's cheekbone, on the center area of her hair and the collar button. Reverse: Some signs of abrasion show on the eagle's neck and the high points on the feathers of the eagle's wings and legs. Virtually all of Mint luster is present.

MS-60: Absolutely no trace of wear permitted. Mint luster may be unattractive, dull or washed out. May have large, detracting contact marks in all areas or damage spots. Rim nicks may be present. May have a patch of or continuous hairline scratches on surfaces. Eye appeal is very poor.

MS-61: Mint luster may be noticeably impaired or diminished. Clusters of large and small contacts marks visible on surface of coin. Hairline scratches may be very noticeable. Scuff marks may be present on major design elements. Small rim nicks and striking or planchet defects may show. Surface quality may be poor and overall eye appeal is somewhat unattractive.

MS-62: Mint luster may be dull or impaired. Clusters of small marks may be present on surfaces and a few large marks or nicks are permitted in the prime focal areas. Hairline scratches are generally very noticeable and large scuff marks may be present on major design elements. Strike, rim and planchet quality may be noticeably below average. Eye appeal overall is generally acceptable.

MS-63: Slight impairment of Mint luster detectable. A few scattered heavy marks and numerous small contact marks permitted. Small hairline scratches visible without magnification. Several scuff marks or detracting defects may be present on design elements or in the fields. General quality of the coin is about average. Overall, the coin is rather attractive.

MS-64: Mint luster and strike are average. Several groups of small contact marks permitted as well as one or two moderately heavy marks. One or two small patches of hairline scratches may be visible under low magnification. Light scuff marks or defects may be detectable on design elements or in the fields. Displays attractive quality and eye appeal is pleasing.

MS-65: Mint luster and strike are attractive and of high quality for the date and Mint facility at which coin was struck. A few small and scattered contact marks or two larger marks permitted. One or two small patches of hairline scratches visible under magnification. Light scuff marks may be detectable on design high points. Quality overall is above average and overall eye appeal is very pleasing.

MS-66: Quality of strike is above average. Full, original Mint luster must be present. No more than two or three noticeable minor contact marks permitted. A few very light hairline scratches may show under magnification or one or two light scuff marks permitted on major design elements or in the fields. Eye appeal must be very pleasing and above average for the date and Mint.

MS-67: Strike is sharp for the date and Mint at which it was struck. Full, original Mint luster present. Three to four very small contact marks and one other noticeable but not detracting mark permitted. One or two small single hairline scratches may show under magnification, or one or two partially hidden scuff marks or flaws may be detectable. Eye appeal is exceptional.

Sacagawea Dollar

Most Sacagawea dollars exist in Uncirculated condition – even the millions that have nominally circulated.

Two factors beyond low circulation contribute to the surprisingly exceptional condition of many Sacagawea dollars.

The first factor is the alloy used to manufacture the Sacagawea planchet. It is among the most wear resistant and the most durable ever created for U.S. coinage.

Long circulation life, while important, was not the Mint's primary goal when it set out to find an alloy for the new dollar coin to be introduced in 2000. Rather, Mint officials were seeking to meet four mandates of the law authorizing issuance of the coin: The coin must be "golden in color," it must have a "distinctive edge," it must be minted and fabricated in the United States, and it must have similar metallic, anti-counterfeiting properties to other circulating U.S. coins.

A copper core planchet with outer layers of an alloy commonly referred to as manganese-brass proved to be the solution. The golden-colored alloy of the outer layers is composed of 77 percent copper, 12 percent zinc, 7 percent manganese and 4 percent nickel.

In addition to looking like 14-karat gold when untoned, the manganese-brass alloy matches the electromagnetic signature of the Anthony dollar – which it was developed to replace. A smooth edge completed the mandates.

Virtually from introduction, the circulation strikes have displayed a wide range in color. Mint officials attribute the change in color to the metamorphosis the alloy undergoes through the annealing process to soften the planchets before striking.

Although the color differences are slight for Uncirculated specimens, they are noticeable and are highly unpredictable. Once in human hands, the Sacagawea dollar coins tend to change color rapidly because the alloy reacts to oils in human skin. The golden color quickly takes on an antique, brownish cast. However, if the coins are handled frequently, the darker patina may wear off the high points of the coin, leaving golden-colored highlights that accent the darker background around the border, lettering and other less exposed areas.

Spotting on the surfaces of many of the more than 1.2 billion Sacagawea dollars produced in 2000 is a problem. Mint officials say a residue left on planchet surfaces during the manufacturing process caused the spotting. The problem was corrected by using a special rinse. Spotting is not apparent on most coins produced beginning in 2001.

The second factor in the high states of preservation for the Sacagawea dollar is low relief. Obverse designer Glenna Goodacre worked under the direction of U.S. Mint Sculptor-Engraver Thomas Rogers (designer of the reverse) to render the low relief required for current circulating coins.

Lack of circulation forced the Mint to halt circulation production after only two years. Beginning with 2002 issues, the business strikes have been produced for the collector market and sold in bags and rolls. However, the smaller production numbers have not produced significantly higher grades. Samples taken from Mint-wrapped rolls of all years indicate the average grades range from Mint State 64 to MS-65. Grades MS-67 and higher tend to be found in special products, such as the Millennium set issued in 2000.

The greatest grading challenge is spying wear on the high points of the design so as to be able to distinguish between About Uncirculated 58 and the first level of Uncirculated, Mint State 60.

Circulation-strike Sacagawea dollars often exhibit numerous contact marks and nicks on Sacagawea's face and neck and also in the fields. Both areas are smooth and easily reveal contact. Scratches on the rim are also common. The eagle's body constitutes the prime focal area on the reverse, but due to the low relief it encounters fewer contact marks.

Most Sacagawea dollars are well or fully struck. Sometimes a slight weakness shows in Sacagawea's hair and on the center of the reverse. Many Sacagawea dollars exhibit satiny to slightly frosty surfaces. Semi-prooflike and prooflike surfaces are frequently encountered.

In the Sacagawea dollar map RED is considered Worst (Average x 4), ORANGE is Bad (Average x 2), YELLOW is Average, GREEN is Better (Average x 1/2) and BLUE is Best (Average x 1/4). A mark in the red area is about eight times more serious than if the same mark is in the green area. The worst places on the obverse for a mark or scratch are on Sacagawea's cheekbone and lower jaw, the Mint mark and date. On the reverse, the worst places for scratches and marks are on the eagle's breast feathers. (Copyright 2005, HeritageCoins.com.)

Design high points on the obverse and the reverse of the Sacagawea dollar are shown in red. Obverse high points include Sacagawea's cheekbone, right eyebrow, nose, jawbone, in her hair near the hairline on the right side of her head, top of her right shoulder, two areas on the center of the doeskin blanket and at the top of Jean-Baptiste's hair above his right forehead. Reverse design high points are on the eagle's neck, breast, lower body feathers, and talons as well as on the edge of the eagle's right wing and along lower regions of primary flight feathers on the eagle's left wing.

AU-58: Slightest trace of wear on design high points. Obverse: Some signs of abrasion detectible on high points of Sacagawea's cheekbone, left eyebrow, nose, jawbone and Jean-Baptiste's hair above left forehead. Reverse: Some signs of abrasion show on eagle's neck, breast, lower body feathers, and talons as well as edge of eagle's right wing and along lower regions of primary flight feathers on left wing. Virtually all of Mint luster is present.

MS-60: Absolutely no trace of wear permitted. Mint luster may be unattractive, dull or washed out. May have large, detracting contact marks in all areas or damage spots. Rim nicks may be present. May have a patch of or continuous hairline scratches on surfaces. Eye appeal is very poor.

MS-61: Mint luster may be noticeably impaired or diminished. Clusters of large and small contact marks visible on surface of coin. Hairline scratches may be very noticeable. Scuff marks may be present on major design elements. Small rim nicks and striking or planchet defects may show. Surface quality may be poor and overall eye appeal is somewhat unattractive.

MS-62: Mint luster may be dull or impaired. Clusters of small marks may be present on surfaces and a few large marks or nicks are permitted in the prime focal areas. Hairline scratches are generally very noticeable and large scuff marks may be present on major design elements. Strike, rim and planchet quality may be noticeably below average. Eye appeal overall is generally acceptable.

MS-63: Slight impairment of Mint luster detectable. A few scattered heavy marks and numerous small contact marks permitted. Small hairline scratches visible without magnification. Several scuff marks or detracting defects may be present on design elements or in the fields. General quality of the coin is about average. Overall, the coin is rather attractive.

MS-64: Mint luster and strike are average. Several groups of small contact marks permitted as well as one or two moderately heavy marks. One or two small patches of hairline scratches may be visible under low magnification. Light scuff marks or defects may be detectable on design elements or in the fields. Displays attractive quality and eye appeal is pleasing.

MS-65: Mint luster and strike are attractive and of high quality for the date and Mint facility at which coin was struck. A few small and scattered contact marks or two larger marks permitted. One or two small patches of hairline scratches are visible under magnification. Light scuff marks may be detectable on design high points. Quality overall is above average and overall eye appeal is very pleasing.

MS-66: Quality of strike is above average. Full, original Mint luster must be present. No more than two or three noticeable minor contact marks permitted. A few very light hairline scratches may show under magnification or one or two light scuff marks permitted on major design elements or in the fields. Eye appeal must be very pleasing and above average for the date and Mint.

MS-67: Strike is sharp for the date and Mint at which it was struck. Full, original Mint luster present. Three to four very small contact marks and one other noticeable but not detracting mark permitted. One or two small single hairline scratches may show under magnification, or one or two partially hidden scuff marks or flaws may be detectable. Eye appeal is exceptional.

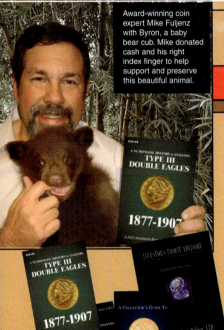

Coronet Double Eagle

Most of the massive amounts of gold extracted from California following the yellow metal's discovery there in 1848 found its way into new, large denomination coins – the $20 double eagle – during the five decades that followed. With a diameter of 1.35 inches, the double eagle was the largest and most valuable U.S. coin issued for circulation.

U.S. Mint Chief Engraver James B. Longacre's obverse design for the double eagle features a left-facing head of Liberty, whose hair is tied in a tight bun with two long curls cascading to the base of her neck. She wears a tiara or coronet inscribed with the legend LIBERTY.

Coronet is the name used to identify Longacre's design in many reference works, although many dealers and collectors routinely refer to it as the Liberty or Liberty Head double eagle, terms commonly used until the latter half of the 20th century.

The obverse has 13 stars around, near the rim. The date is centered below the base of Liberty's neck.

The reverse features a left-facing heraldic eagle with a shield covering his body. In his beak he holds a ribbon sporting the E PLURIBUS UNUM legend. In his right talons he holds an olive branch signifying a desire for peace; in his left talon he holds arrows, denoting a readiness to defend freedom. A circle of small stars is above the eagle's head and

the sun's rays rise toward the legend UNITED STATES OF AMERICA. The value of the coin is situated below the eagle, expressed as TWENTY D. on the first version of the reverse.

The original design, produced from 1850 to 1866, is known today by its "No Motto" reverse, often denoted as Type I. This design was struck at minting facilities in Philadelphia, San Francisco and New Orleans.

The motto IN GOD WE TRUST was added in the circle of stars on the reverse in 1866, hence it is described as the "With Motto" design, which was struck at the Philadelphia, San Francisco and Carson City Mints through 1876. It is often referred to as Type II.

Beginning in 1877, the denomination on the reverse was spelled out as TWENTY DOLLARS, leading to a third subtype: the "With Motto, Twenty Dollars" reverse or Type III. It was struck at five minting facilities – Philadelphia, San Francisco, Carson City, New Orleans and Denver – and was last issued in 1907.

A key to grading this large gold coin is the LIBERTY legend on the coronet. The legend is not as recessed in this design as it is on other denominations with the Liberty Head or Coronet design. Hence, the legend wears more quickly, especially the letters RTY. However, look closely because the coin may have been weakly struck and the weakness manifests in this region of the design. You may be observing a

weak strike rather than wear. Look for breaks in the luster to confirm wear. If the luster is intact, it is a weak strike.

If there is wear, it will be evident on the high points of the design: On the obverse, the highest points are Liberty's hair above her forehead, her eyebrow and her central cheek area; on the reverse, the highest points are the tips of the eagle's wings and the feathers on the eagle's neck.

Unless they are rare dates or varieties, few Coronet double eagles are encountered in the today's marketplace that grade below About Uncirculated 50 to Extremely Fine 45. The reason is simple. Coins grading mid-AU to higher AU and in the first four grades of Mint State are readily available, especially in dates after 1866.

Professional graders suggest that with normal eyesight, grading should be done without magnification. Because of the large-size canvas and open fields, Coronet double eagles typically exhibit many contact marks – even the Uncirculated specimens.

So many of these old gold coins have been cleaned or lightly dipped through the years that today's market rewards original surfaces and great eye appeal, especially in the higher ranges of Mint State.

In Mint State 65 and higher grades, the brilliance of the luster is most often the most important factor in grade assignment.

In the Coronet double eagle map RED is considered Worst (Average x 4), ORANGE is Bad (Average x 2), YELLOW is Average, GREEN is Better (Average x 1/2) and BLUE is Best (Average x 1/4). A mark in the red area is about eight times more serious than if the same mark is in the green area. The worst places on the obverse for a mark or scratch are on Liberty's face and on the date. On the reverse, the worst places for scratches and marks are on the eagle's head and the lower part of the shield. (Copyright 1990, HeritageCoins.com.)

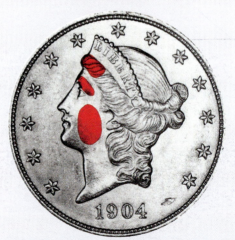

Design high points on the obverse and the reverse of the Coronet $20 double eagle are highlighted in red. The highest points on the obverse are on Liberty's hair above her forehead, her eyebrow and her central cheek area. On the reverse, the highest points are the tips of the eagle's wings and the feathers on the eagle's neck.

EF-45: Light wear detectable on high points of design. Obverse: Light wear on Liberty's cheek and hair below the coronet, above her ear and curls below her ear, and on prongs of coronet. Contact marks in field and some wear shows on stars. All letters of LIBERTY on coronet complete, although slight weakness or wear on last three letters may show. Reverse: Eagle's wing feathers show detail. Light wear across the eagle, shield and scroll. Some Mint luster present.

AU-53: Light wear shows on design high points. Obverse: Noticeable wear and contact marks in fields. Slight wear on Liberty's cheek, eyebrow, on hair on forehead below the coronet and on the coronet. All letters of LIBERTY are strong. Reverse: Slight wear on eagle's body, shield and scroll. Half of Mint luster present.

AU-55: Slightest trace of wear present on highest points of the design. Obverse: Trace of wear visible on Liberty's cheek and hair. Reverse: Trace of wear visible on eagle's wingtips, neck and tail feathers, and on high points of scroll. Three-fourths of Mint luster present.

Coronet Double Eagle

AU-58: Some signs of wear detectable on the highest points of the design. Obverse: Abrasions detectable on Liberty's hair and coronet. Reverse: Slight abrasions detectable on eagle's neck and wing tips, and on top of shield.

MS-60: Uncirculated. Absolutely no trace of wear permitted. Mint luster may be unattractive, dull or washed out. May have large, detracting contact marks in all areas or damage spots. Rim nicks may be present. May have a patch of or continuous hairline scratches on surfaces. Eye appeal is very poor.

MS-61: Uncirculated. Mint luster may be noticeably impaired or diminished. Clusters of large and small contact marks visible on surface of coin. Hairline scratches may be very noticeable. Scuff marks may be present on major design elements. Small rim nicks and striking or planchet defects may show. Surface quality may be poor and overall eye appeal is somewhat unattractive.

MS-62: Uncirculated. Mint luster may be dull or impaired. Clusters of small marks may be present on surfaces and a few large marks or nicks are permitted in the prime focal areas. Hairline scratches are generally very noticeable and large scuff marks may be present on major design elements. Strike, rim and planchet quality may be noticeably below average. Eye appeal overall is generally acceptable.

MS-63: Uncirculated. Slight impairment of Mint luster detectable. A few scattered heavy marks and numerous small contact marks permitted. Small hairline scratches visible without magnification. Several scuff marks or detracting defects may be present on design elements or in the fields. General quality of the coin is about average. Overall, the coin is rather attractive.

MS-64: Uncirculated. Mint luster and strike are average. Several groups of small contact marks permitted as well as one or two moderately heavy marks. One or two small patches of hairline scratches may be visible under low magnification. Light scuff marks or defects may be detectable on design elements or in the fields. Displays attractive quality, and eye appeal is pleasing.

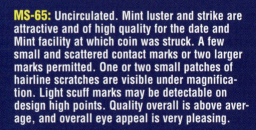

MS-65: Uncirculated. Mint luster and strike are attractive and of high quality for the date and Mint facility at which coin was struck. A few small and scattered contact marks or two larger marks permitted. One or two small patches of hairline scratches are visible under magnification. Light scuff marks may be detectable on design high points. Quality overall is above average, and overall eye appeal is very pleasing.

MS-66: Uncirculated. Quality of strike is above average. Full, original Mint luster must be present. No more than two or three noticeable minor contact marks permitted. A few very light hairline scratches may show under magnification or one or two light scuff marks permitted on major design elements or in the fields. Eye appeal must be very pleasing and above average for the date and Mint.

Coin Values:
The one price guide you can rely on.

Compare *Coin Values* with any other pricing guide and hands down, we're the most comprehensive one out there. 45,000+ U.S. coin values and counting.

But we know you don't only care about sheer numbers.

You're looking for information you can trust. Information you can interpret quickly. Information you can use.

And that's what really sets us apart from the rest: The little things we do to ensure that.

For starters, every value you see is the result of thorough research. We carefully examine a variety of sources: actual transactions, public auctions, fixed-price lists, and more.

And we do it often. Need the most current prices? Between monthly print issues, we update prices as much as once a week and make them available to you online at www.coinvaluesonline.com.

Not a current Coin Values subscriber? Subscribe to Coin Values today and save 27% off the newsstand price!
12 issues $36.95

FACT: Coin Values provides twice as many values as any other coin pricing guide available today.

FACT: Coin Values provides comprehensive listings for higher grades. Other guides don't.

FACT: Only Coin Values has full-color coin images, each the actual size of the coin. Obverse and reverse. This helps our readers quickly identify coins.

Name _____

Address _____

City _____ State _____ Zip _____

May we contact you by email. ☐ Yes   ☐ No

Email address _____

Canada add $15 per year for postage. All other foreign countries add $30 per year for postage. Offer expires 2/28/06. Mail to: Coin Values, PO Box 747, Sidney OH 45365-0747   T95GBK

Saint-Gaudens Double Eagle

The relatively large size of the Saint-Gaudens gold $20 double eagle (34.29 millimeters or 1.35 inches in diameter) makes its among the easiest in the U.S. series to grade.

Produced from 1907 to 1933, the coin takes its name from its designer, Augustus Saint-Gaudens.

The obverse depicts a Striding Liberty figure holding high in her right hand the torch of freedom, an olive branch in her outstretched left hand. With the rays of a rising sun at her back, Liberty steps into the future with her right foot on solid ground and her left foot landing on a rocky ledge. The date is to the right of the rock and above a branch of oak, which appears to spring from the coin's lower right border. A tiny U.S. Capitol dome is nestled on the lower left side of the coin, just under Liberty's flowing skirt. Stars ring the outer border of the coin. Letters in the LIBERTY legend are widely spaced and appear at the top, above Liberty's head.

The reverse design depicts a side view of an eagle in flight, its head on the left side of the coin. The eagle flies atop a sun with rays radiating upward.

"Saints" began as a high-relief design. While pleasing to the eye, the design proved impractical for commerce. The high relief required multiple blows of the dies to fully form the designs. The relief also caused problems in stacking. The Mint remedied the problem by lowering the relief in mid-1907. The relief change flattened Miss Liberty's left knee, a key design high point on the obverse. The engraver also changed the date from Roman numerals to Arabic numerals.

When grading, it's important to know that flat knees on the 1907 Saint-Gaudens, Arabic Numerals double eagles are a result of lowering the relief on the design. Generally flatness on a design element can be attributed to weak strike or wear. But one has to become acquainted with how the low-relief flatness should look and then check for evidence of wear on these early Saint-Gaudens $20 coins.

The flatness of the knees was a short-lived problem. In 1908 when the Mint added the motto IN GOD WE TRUST on the reverse, it used the redesign opportunity to make Liberty's knee more rounded. (The Philadelphia Mint and Denver Mint versions of the 1908 coins exist in both No Motto and With Motto subtypes; the San Francisco Mint coin appears as a With Motto subtype only.)

Because Saint-Gaudens' detailed designs use the entire canvas, nicks, scratches and minor blemishes are harder to detect than on large portrait coins with open fields. However, rotating the coin under light easily reveals these problems to the naked eye.

Begin the grading process by first inspecting the design high points for evidence of wear. Tilt and rotate the coin, looking for a contrast of luster between the high points and the rest of the coin. Look for dullness or a difference in color on design high points, which signals loss of original luster.

Marks created by counting machines, referred to as "wheel marks," are frequently encountered on Saint-Gaudens double eagles and appear to be concentrated patches of hairline scratches. Some grading services will not grade Saint-Gaudens gold $20 coins exhibiting severe wheel marks.

With regard to strike, the 1907 and 1908 Saint-Gaudens, Arabic Numerals, No Motto double eagles usually exhibit flatness on the Liberty's breasts, left knee and leg. There is usually some flatness evident on Liberty's head and nose. Also, the torch and olive branch can appear flat. On the reverse the upper part of the eagle's wings and his entire body, including his tail and claws, tend to be flat. The top part of the sun and some of the rays also sometimes are weakly struck.

Coins struck beginning in 1908 that carry the motto are slightly more rounded in all of these key areas but weakness of strike is still evident in the same areas as the earlier strikes sans the motto.

In the Saint-Gaudens double eagle map RED is considered Worst (Average x 4), ORANGE is Bad (Average x 2), YELLOW is Average, GREEN is Better (Average x 1/2) and BLUE is Best (Average x 1/4). A mark in the red area is about eight times more serious than if the same mark is in the green area. The worst places on the obverse for a mark or scratch are on Liberty's head, her left arm, her body to just below her knees and the date. On the reverse, the worst places for scratches and marks are on the eagle's head and breast feathers. (Copyright 1990, HeritageCoins.com.)

Wear is detected first on the high points of the coin's design, which are highlighted in red. The highest points on the obverse are on Liberty's breasts and her left knee. The highest points on the reverse are the eagle's breast and the leading edge of his left wing. (Copyright 1990, HeritageCoins.com.)

AU-50: On the obverse, wear detectable on Liberty's breasts, left knee and nose. Wear apparent also in the fields. On the reverse, wear noticeable on the eagle's breast, lower body and upper wing feathers. Friction present in fields on both obverse and reverse, except in protected areas. Half of the original Mint luster is present. Deep or long contact marks may drop coin from the AU grade range.

AU-55: Small traces of wear visible on highest points of the design. On the obverse, wear visible on Liberty's left breast, left knee, forehead and nose. Reverse: Trace of wear obvious on eagle's wing feathers. Slight friction evident in the fields. Three-quarters of original Mint luster is present.

AU-58: Smallest trace of wear detectable on Liberty's left breast, and knee. Reverse: Barely visible wear on eagle's upper wing, body and breast. More than three-fourths of original Mint luster is present.

MS-60: Strictly Uncirculated, no trace of wear. May have heavy contact marks in all areas. May have noticeable patch or continuous hairline scratches on both sides. Luster may be impaired or original. Eye appeal is generally poor.

MS-61: Uncirculated, no trace of wear. May have some heavy or many light contact marks in both the prime and secondary focal areas on both the obverse and reverse. May have apparent hairline scratches on both the obverse and reverse. Luster may be impaired or original; coin is generally unattractive.

MS-62: Uncirculated, no trace of wear. May have a few distracting contact marks in prime and secondary focal areas. May have a few scattered or patches of hairline scratches. Luster may be original or impaired. Has generally acceptable eye appeal.

MS-63: Uncirculated, no trace of wear. May have a few distracting contact marks in prime focal area. May have a few scattered or a small patch of hairline scratches. Luster may be slightly impaired or original. Coin is generally attractive.

MS-64: Uncirculated, no trace of wear. May have a few light, scattered contact marks with some in prime focal areas. May have a few hairline scratches in secondary focal areas. Luster should be average, fully original. Coin has pleasing eye appeal.

MS-65: Uncirculated, no trace of wear. May have light, scattered contact marks but none in the prime focal areas. May have a few, light and scattered hairline scratches. Luster is fully original. Coin has overall very pleasing eye appeal.

PREMIER COIN HOLDERS

- Size and style match perfectly with PCGS-style certified holders.
- Hard acrylic case offers unsurpassed optical clarity and security. It is notched for easy access to insert.
- Archival-quality insert that is PVC free and completely inert.

Sold in packages of three

Retail $5.99   AA* **$4.99**

ITEM	DESCRIPTION
CWCH01	**U.S. Half Cents** (Size: .93"/23.5mm in diameter)
CWCH02	**U.S. Two Cents & Smaller Half Cents** (Size: .91"/23mm in diameter)
CWCH03	**U.S. Coronet Large Cent** (Size: 1.10"/27.5mm in diameter)
CWCH04	**U.S. Large Cents** (Size: 1.13"/28.5-29mm in diameter)
CWCH05	**U.S. Flying Eagle, Indian & Lincoln Head Cents** (Size: .75"/19.05-19.3mm in diameter)
CWCH06	**U.S. Liberty Head, Indian Head & Jefferson Nickels** (Size: .84"/21.21mm in diameter)
CWCH07	**U.S. Shield Nickel, Indian Head $3 Gold** (Size: .81"/20.50mm in diameter)
CWCH08	**U.S. Capped Bust & Seated Liberty Half Dimes** (Size: .61"/15.50mm in diameter)
CWCH09	**U.S. 3¢ Copper Nickel; Seated Liberty, Barber, Winged Liberty, Roosevelt Dimes; Coronet & Indian Head $2.50 Gold Quarters Eagles** (Size: .7-.72"/17.78-18.2mm in diameter)
CWCH10	**U.S. Capped Bust (1831-38), Seated Liberty Barber, Standing Liberty & Washington Quarters** (Size: .96"/24.26mm in diameter)
CWCH11	**U.S. Flowing Hair, Draped Bust & Capped Bust (1807-36) Half Dollars; 1oz. Gold & Platinum American Eagles** (Size: 1.28-1.29"/32.5-32.7mm in diameter)
CWCH12	**U.S. Capped Bust (1836-39), Seated Liberty, Barber, Walking Liberty, Franklin and Kennedy Half Dollars** (Size: 1.21"/30.61mm in diameter)
CWCH13	**U.S. Seated Liberty, Trade, Morgan, Peace & Eisenhower Dollars** (Size: 1.5"/38.1mm in diameter)
CWCH14	**U.S. Anthony & Sacagawea Dollars** (Size: 1.05"/26.5mm in diameter)
CWCH15	**U.S. Coronet & Indian Head $5 Gold Half Eagles** (Size: .85"/21.54mm in diameter)
CWCH16	**U.S. Flowing Hair & Draped Bust Half Dimes** (Size: .65"/16.5mm in diameter)
CWCH17	**U.S. ¼ oz. Gold & Platinum American Eagles** (Size: .87"/22mm in diameter)
CWCH18	**U.S. Coronet & Indian Head $10 Gold Eagles; ½ oz. Gold & Platinum American Eagles** (Size: 1.07"/27mm in diameter)
CWCH19	**U.S. Coronet & St. Gaudens $20 Gold Double Eagles** (Size: 1.35"/34.29mm in Diameter)
CWCH20	**U.S. 1 oz. Silver American Eagles** (Size: 1.58"/40.1mm in diameter)
CWCH21	**U.S. 20¢ Smaller Half Cents** (Size: .885 - 89"/22.6mm in diameter)
CWCH22	**Larger U.S. Large Cents** (Size: 1.135"/29mm in diameter)
CWCH23	**Smaller U.S. $20 Double Eagles** (Size: 1.315"/33.4mm in diameter)
CWCH24	**Smaller U.S. Silver Dollars** (Size: 1.465"/37.2mm in diameter)
CWCH25	**Smaller U.S. Peace Dollars** (Size: 1.495"/37.9mm in diameter)
CWCH26	**U.S. Three Cents Silver** (Size: .55"/14mm in diameter)
CWCH27	**U.S. Draped Bust, Capped Bust (1809-37) Dimes** (Size: .74"/18.8mm in diameter)
CWCH28	**U.S. Coronet Gold Dollar** (Size: .51"/13mm in diameter)
CWCH29	**U.S. Indian Head Gold Dollar** (Size: .59"/14.9mm in diameter)

To Order Call 1-800-572-6885

ITEM	DESCRIPTION
CWCH30	**U.S. 1/10 oz Gold American Eagle** (Size: .657"/16.58mm in diameter)
CWCH32	**Canada 50¢ (1870-1967)** (Size: 1.17"/29.7mm in diameter)
CWCH33	**Canada Silver Dollar (1935-1967)** (Size: 1.417"/36mm in diameter)
CWCH34	**Great Britain Crown (1818-2003)** (Size: 1.52"/38.6mm in diameter)
CWCH35	**Canada Dime** (Size: 18.08mm/0.712" in diameter)
CWCH36	**Canada 1/4 oz. Maple Leaf** (Size: 20mm/0.788" in diameter)
CWCH37	**Canada 1/2 oz. Maple Leaf** (Size: 24.9mm/0.984" in diameter)
CWCH38	**Canada 1 oz. Maple Leaf** (Size: 1.18/30.1mm in diameter)
CWCH39	**1 oz. Gold & Platinum American Eagles** (Size: 1.29/32.7mm in diameter)

TAG WIZARD KIT

Create professional look-ing identification tags for your Coin World coin holders using the Tag Wizard software. Kit includes software and 1,875 Coin World self-adhesive ID tags in sheets of 75. Additional sheets of tags sold separately.

ITEM	RETAIL	AA*
SATAGKIT	$27.99	**$19.99**

TAGWIZARD 2.0 SOFTWARE ONLY

ITEM	RETAIL	AA*
TAGWIZ	$12.99	**$9.99**

SELF-ADHESIVE ID TAGS - 25 sheets, 1,875 tags.

ITEM	RETAIL	AA*
CWIDTGSA	$15.99	**$13.99**

Save on pre-packaged sets!

Save on both the case and coin holders when you order complete Coin World Storage sets! Sets feature the handsome acrylic Coin World Coin Case filled with 24 specific coin holders and ID tags.

PREMIER SETS

ITEM	DESCRIPTION	HOLDERS	RETAIL	AA*
CWCH05PS	**Cent Set**	24	$56.99	**$42.99**
CWCH06PS	**Nickel Set**	24	$56.99	**$42.99**
CWCH09PS	**Dime Set**	24	$56.99	**$42.99**
CWCH10PS	**Quarters Set**	25	$56.99	**$42.99**
CWCH12PS	**Half Dollar Set**	24	$56.99	**$42.99**
CWCH13PS	**Silver Dollar Set**	24	$56.99	**$42.99**
CWCH20PS	**Silver Eagle Set**	24	$56.99	**$42.99**
CWCHPBAS	**Basic Assorted Set**	18	$44.99	**$24.99**

1 Pack of Cent, Nickel, Dime, Quarter, Half Dollar and Silver Dollar holders plus Coin World Coin Case.

CWCHPKIT	**Starter Kit**	240	$574.99	**$449.99**

80 packs of Coin World Premier Holders plus 10 Premier Coin World Coin Cases.

COIN WORLD COIN HOLDERS COIN CASE

Attractive acrylic case will hold up to 25 Coin World coin holders.

ITEM		RETAIL	AA*
CWCSE02P	Premier Coin Case	$9.99	**$7.99**

FOUR & FIVE-COIN SET HOLDERS

Enjoy the convenience the Coin World Slab style holders have to offer in a 4 and 5-coin mint and proof set holders.

4-COIN HOLDER SETS

ITEM	DESCRIPTION	RETAIL	AA*
CWGOLD4	U.S. Gold (Liberty or Indian Gold coins)	$4.49	**$3.49**
CWGBLN4	U.S. Gold Bullion	$4.49	**$3.49**
CWNKLSET4	U.S. Nickel	$4.49	**$3.49**

5-COIN HOLDER SETS

ITEM	DESCRIPTION	RETAIL	AA*
CWPRFSET	U.S. Proof Set (Cent - Half Dollar)	$4.99	**$3.89**
CWMNTSET	U.S. Mint Set (Cent - Half Dollar)	$4.99	**$3.89**
CWQTRSET	State Quarter Set	$4.99	**$3.89**
CWCENTSET	U.S. Cent Type Set	$4.99	**$3.89**
CWNKLSET5	U.S. Nickel Type Set	$4.99	**$3.89**
CWJFNKLS5	Jefferson Nickel	$4.99	**$3.89**

STATE QUARTER STORAGE SET

Includes Premier Coin case and the 5 State Quarter set holders.

ITEM	RETAIL	AA*
CWQTRBOX	$32.99	**$24.99**

1. AA prices apply to paid subscribers of Amos Hobby Publishing titles.
2. Prices, terms and product availability subject to change.

Online at www.amosadvantage.com

AMOS ADVANTAGE

AD INDEX

AMERICAN NUMISMATIC ASSOCIATION

YES! Make me a member of America's Coin Club. I will receive the ANA's award-winning monthly journal, *Numismatist,* access to the ANA library and educational programs, and many other exclusive member benefits.

MEMBERSHIP

❍ Regular, $39*

❍ Senior, $35*

* Includes one-time $6 application fee.

EXTEND YOUR MEMBERSHIP!

❍ 3-year Regular (save $15), $90

❍ 3-year Senior (save $14), $79

NAME

ADDRESS

CITY _____ STATE _____ ZIP

DATE OF BIRTH _____ E-MAIL

SIGNATURE   CVGUIDE

I herewith make application for membership in the American Numismatic Association, subject to the bylaws of the Association. I also agree to abide by the Code of Ethics adopted by the Association.

PLEASE CHARGE MY:

❍ Visa   ❍ Mastercard

❍ AmEx   ❍ Discover

❍ Periodically, the ANA's mailing list is rented or provided to third parties. If you do not want your information provided for non-ANA-related mailings, please check here. Previous requests not to provide your information will continue to be honored.

CARD NUMBER _____ - _____ EXPIRATION DATE

Make check payable to the American Numismatic Association. Please send to ANA, 818 N. Cascade Ave., Colorado Springs, CO 80903, fax 719-634-4085, phone 800-514-2646, or join at www.money.org.

AMERICAN NUMISMATIC ASSOCIATION